HIDDEN TREASURE IN THE PSALMS

HIDDEN TREASURE IN THE WALLS

HIDDEN TREASURE
IN THE PSALMS

by

RUDOLF FRIELING

The original translation by Mabel Cotterell revised, and with six
additional chapters translated by A. Heidenreich and E. Hersey

Second enlarged edition

1967

THE CHRISTIAN COMMUNITY PRESS
34 Glenilla Road, London, N.W.3

First Edition 1954

The illustration on the cover of this book is of an Iraq-Ischali terracotta plaque reproduced by kind permission of the Oriental Institute, University of Chicago. The cover has been designed by Mairis Wittkowski-Macdonald.

PRINTED IN GREAT BRITAIN BY EBENEZER BAYLIS AND SON, LIMITED
THE TRINITY PRESS, WORCESTER, AND LONDON

Contents

Translators' Foreword

Among the Jews of the Old Testament humanity learned to pray. The Psalms are the first and oldest collection of prayers of the human race. The ancient sacred scriptures of oriental religions include incantations but no prayers. The Greeks of Homer's time, approximately contemporary with King David, had beliefs in gods but they did not pray. Prayer, the intimate, personal communication between an I and a Thou in adoration, petition, confession and ultimate surrender was born among the Jews.

It was part of the fruits of monotheism, which, fully understood, is not an abstract belief in One God, but a profound realization of the unity of the Spirit World. The people of the Old Testament were the first to be aware of this unity, centred in One Divine Being, because they were first aware of the essential unity of the human soul, centred in a self, a spiritual Ego. The experience of the microcosmic human unity opened the vision for the macrocosmic Divine Unity and vice versa.

The history of the Jewish people is the story of this development and discovery. They were the forerunners, representatives and custodians for the whole human race of the process of the emerging Ego in man. They produced and maintained the racial characteristics of a type of body in which the realization of an Ego could first take place. But they bore also the brunt of that delicate and tragic process of the Ego separating itself while maintaining its link and even identity with God. They were engaged as a race and as a nation in a spiritual-moral problem which has ever since been the problem and task facing every individual human being. In this process of finding himself, the devout man of the Old Testament found also his way to a personal God whose mysterious, unutterable name was I AM, and again his way back from this God to man.

In the Psalms we share in this growth, which in some way or other is also our own most personal concern. We overhear the music, the sighs, the harmonies and disharmonies of the process. We listen to the exultations of the soul who has found God, to the cries of despair in abandonment and sin; we grasp the significance of the Law as the indispensable "schoolmaster" and the rejection of those who refuse to accept its discipline. Because of their central and universal human character, the Psalms have exercised a greater influence than almost any other book of the Bible. Among those who have guided the destinies of nations many knew the Psalms practically by heart. The spirit, poetic flavour and religious sentiment of the Psalms are deeply integrated into the popular consciousness of the Western World.

But a new generation is rising, which looks with critical eyes at all things biblical, and which does no longer accept inherited spiritual treasures for granted. Its apparent indifference is not altogether due to lack of interest, but often to the lack of a rational access to understanding. The spiritual legacy of the past needs a new appraisal and a new presentation freed from associations with outdated religious doctrines.

Rudolf Frieling's studies in the Psalms provide just this. Even some of the best-known Psalms, like 23 or 90, whose very familiarity may obscure their full meaning and prevent newcomers from taking an interest, reveal unsuspected treasures under Dr. Frieling's delicate and searching treatment. This is why the translators thought that they should make these Studies available to English-speaking people, and this all the more so, because perhaps nowhere else in the world have the Psalms been so deeply absorbed into the very foundations of the national consciousness than among the great family of English-speaking peoples at home and overseas.

Rudolf Frieling draws on two special sources for these Studies. The one is his own Hebrew scholarship and, if we may say so, his very original and fresh approach. His second source is the philosophical and theological background of *The Christian Community*, the international Movement for Religious Renewal which came

into being in 1922 with the help and advice of the late Rudolf
Steiner, the founder of Anthroposophy. The teaching of that
"Scientist of the Invisible" is never used by Dr. Frieling in any
dogmatic way. But Steiner's unique insight into the spiritual
climate and consciousness of past Ages, and his grasp of the whole
range of supra-sensory experience in the religions of the world,
offer an enormous help for the understanding of sacred literature
which contains frequently more of "occult" elements than a
modern reader at first realizes.

In the original German Dr. Frieling uses on occasion anthropo-
sophical terms. When speaking of the human being in his four-
fold nature, he speaks of the Ego, as the individual spiritual self,
he refers at times to the soul and the whole range of emotions as
the "astral" nature of man, and to the phenomena of life as the
"etheric" world. Dealing with the powers of evil, he accepts
Steiner's conception of the duality of evil and uses in addition to
the biblical phrases "Devil" and "Satan", the terms "Lucifer"
(Devil) and Ahriman (Satan). Readers may also wonder in what
sense Christ is described in one or two places as "The Spirit of the
Sun". This is, of course, in accordance with ancient wisdom,
approached afresh and independently by Rudolf Steiner, which
perceived beyond the material Sun an invisible but real sphere of
living energy, from which all living Truth, Beauty and Goodness
are inspired. Although English readers may at first be slightly
more puzzled by these terms than German readers, the translators
thought that these terms should be kept and not transcribed.

The translators are greatly indebted to Miss Mabel Cotterell,
O.B.E. for the translation of the earlier and shorter edition of
1956. As a number of new chapters have been added to this
second edition, we thought it right, however, to revise the original translation, as it turned out rather thoroughly, in order to pro-
duce something of a unified style for the whole book. The Studies
on Psalms 22, 46, 65, 84, 96 and 110 appeared first in The Christian Community Magazine and we express our gratitude to the
Editor for permission to include them in this edition.

London, Easter 1967   A.H. E.H.

Man under the Stars

I

In the season of autumn we can "come to ourselves" more readily than at any other time of the year. During the summer sun and heat often threaten to oppress us, in winter cold and darkness cast their spell. In spring the fresh new life tends to carry us away. But in the cool of autumn man returns to himself. In the sign of the scales—the zodiacal sign of autumn—he finds his balance.

Psalm 8 is an autumnal contemplation. Very likely the Hebrew text suggests as subtitle "a song at the winepress", not "a song upon the Gitthit" (a musical instrument) as the Authorized Version has it. The Septuagint, the Greek translation of the Old Testament, made in the third century B.C. for the Jews of the dispersion, also interpreted the instruction as referring to the wine-making, an activity well-known to the Greeks and traditionally accompanied with special songs and hymns. The picture of the ripe green and golden grapes forms the background of our Psalm, in which the mysterious position of man is weighed, as he is poised between heaven and earth.

Valuable discoveries are made when we observe how each language has its special designation for "Man". Thus, for instance, the English *man* and the German *Mensch* are both connected with an indo-germanic word which indicates *thought, thinking*. Here man is recognized above all beings as the bearer of the spirit.

An-thropos in Greek means "the one who looks upward"; it is felt essential that he is capable of looking upward to heaven, that he can lift his eyes to the stars. *Homo, humanus* in Latin is related to *humus;* hence he is the terrestrial, the earthly, he who stands in a distinct and important connection with the earth. The Hebrew agrees here with the Latin. In the language of the Old Testament the human being is fundamentally characterized through his earthly relationship. *Adamah* is the Earth, *Adam,* the human being. Man is thus felt to be one who is unthinkable without the specifically terrestrial earthly element. He is closely connected with the whole evolution of the earth, he is its crown and completion.

This Earth-aspect of man is of greatest significance. Man is the goal and meaning of the Earth. He bears in himself the extract of its finest forces. Only under the quite special and peculiar conditions of earthly existence can man evolve to an independent personality endowed with ego-consciousness. Yet however justifiable the Roman-Hebrew name for man may be, it needs completion. It can lead to the one-sidedness of materialism if only man's relation to the earth is stressed. The other aspect is wonderfully brought into play through the Greek aspect: *anthropos,* the one looking upward.

On the one hand it is true that no independent ego-consciousness is possible without passing through the hard sphere of the terrestrial. But it must not be forgotten that what presses through to self-consciousness against the resistance of earthly conditions originates from above. And when man looks up to the stars he lifts himself to the sublime worlds of his heavenly origin. Here too there is the danger of one-sidedness, drastically expressed in the story of the philosopher who contemplates the heavens and falls into a ditch because he has paid no attention to his path on earth.

It is only in harmony between Above and Below, between Heaven and Earth that the true being of man is achieved. As Goethe put it:

" 'Twixt the Over, 'twixt the Under
Hover I to lively view,
I rejoice in colour-wonder,
I refresh myself in blue.
If by day blue mountain distance

Ardently attracts my sight,
Starry splendour's superfluence
Glows above my head at night.
Thus I daily, thus I nightly
Glory in the lot of man.
When he finds the right by thinking
He is ever great and fine."

"What is man?" In the 8th Psalm this question is formally posed, and in a wonderful assessment of his heavenly and earthly importance, the nature of man is set forth and extolled.

> Lord, our Lord,
> How gloriously is the splendour of Thy name
> reflected by all the earth.

The earth is a realm of divine manifestation. "How is thy Name visibly inscribed in all earth-existence!" The earth is thus not only dull heavy substance, blind and deaf. It is not only anonymous matter, accidental assembly of nameless atoms. On the contrary, it is filled with the divine Name. The "name" is the inner nature, the essence, lifted into consciousness of what is known of a being. So the "Name of God" is the tenor and purport of what the Divinity gives of itself to be known. In the individual works of creation the letters of this divine Name are, as it were, the open secret. Hence the Name shines forth out of earth-existence.

In the same breath the Psalm passes over from the earthly to the heavenly, and so our eyes are raised to the upper world:

> Thou hast poured out Thy majesty
> throughout the heavens.

The earth, weighty with the secrets of the great Name, is arched over by the spheres of heaven. The word "heaven" in Hebrew is plural. At that time men still knew of the supersensible worlds ranging upward one beyond another and turning to us their "outer side" in the firmament of stars. St. Paul, for instance, speaks of being "caught up" into the "third heaven"

(2 Cor. 12; 2). The reflection of the Name in the earth guides our gaze upwards to the heavens in which the Godhead is revealed in eternal radiation. This raising and lowering of our eyes to heaven and to earth continues, as we shall see, to be characteristic of the 8th Psalm.

From the outspread radiation in the heavens let us turn again to earth. Now for the first time Man appears in the field of vision, and first in the stage of childhood:

> *Out of the mouth of babes and sucklings hast*
> *thou established a power against Thy*
> *oppressors, to silence the adversary and the*
> *rebellious.*

From the modern intellectual point of view the child is just a not yet fully-grown man, a "not yet". In contrast to this the grown-up person, measured by the child, represents in many respects a "no longer". He is by no means only the goal, the attainment of which "devalues" the preceding stages. No; childhood has its own intrinsic worth. From the purely earthly point of view, the child, as a still young inhabitant of earth, is imperfection, immaturity. Adding, however, the heavenly standpoint, childhood is highly significant. For the child is the not yet completely incarnated human being, one who still belongs in a great measure to the higher worlds. "Their angels do always behold the face of my Father which is in heaven" (Matt. 18; 10). It is significant that in the 8th Psalm the words about children are placed between verses 2 and 4, both of which contemplate the starry heavens.

If we recognize the heavenly in addition to the earthly we no longer see in the child merely the still unfinished adult. We are no longer tempted to "offend these little ones". Indeed, we recognize in the nature of the child a powerful factor in the duel which is fought around men by good and evil spirits.

Infinitely much spirituality would be lost if man came into the world at once clever and grown-up, fixed and finished, without being first a child. Few people have any idea how much they have to thank the twilight years of childhood for those moments when they were gently touched by a higher world. Powerful divine forces continuously enter earthly existence through experience of one's own childhood, or the childhood stage of others. How much light and warmth has been shed by the picture of the Christ-Child in the crib into a grown-up world which has grown cold. So we can take quite seriously the Psalmist's words, that for the Godhead the stage of human childhood represents in its own right a factor of strength in the conflict with the opposing powers. These are the forces of the Adversary who would tear from the heart of earthly man the memory of his heavenly origin and thus turn him into a mere creature of earth. Mere earthly intellectuality is in its very nature unchildlike. It makes one precocious and so plays into the hands of the powers of death.

"A power against thine oppressors." The oppressors (this is the literal translation) are in fact the beings who drive the divine element on earth "into a corner"; they wish to deprive it of room to live and air to breathe in. This passage in the Psalms once falls also from the lips of Christ. The High Priests and Scribes take offence at the Hosanna which the children in the Temple cried out to Him on His entry. Christ answers them with the words of Psalm 8; 3 (Matt. 21; 15, 16). With the Christ the lost and forgotten heaven draws once more into the world of man; and it is the childlike element in the people, which in contrast to the inwardly fossilized High Priests and Scribes recognizes the One Who is entering and hails Him with cries of joy.

From the sphere of childhood the gaze of Psalm 8 turns upward again:

> When I consider the heavens, the work of thy
> hands, the moon and the stars which thou hast
> established . . .

Here the Greek aspect of man is most beautifully shown: *anthropos*, the one who looks upwards. Above all earthly needs and riches we look with deep awe into the splendour of the star-set night sky. The Psalms do not often speak of the stars. The word "star" (*Kokab*) is not to be found again till towards the end of the

Book of Psalms. In Psalm 136 the works of Creation are enumerated, each sentence being followed by the response: "For his
mercy endureth for ever." All the separate acts of creation in
Genesis are brought once more to consciousness and extolled as
proofs of mercy, communications of divine spiritual life. "Who
made the great lights—for his mercy endureth for ever; the sun
to rule by day—for his mercy endureth for ever; the moon and
the stars to rule by night—for his mercy endureth for ever."

Then in Psalm 147; 4: "He telleth the number of the stars; he
calleth them all by their names". The numbering does not signify
mere calculation. Its purport is that God carries them all in His
consciousness, and indeed as organism of a totality, as a complete
choir. But this entirety (the number) consists again of purely
separate star-individualities, as St. Paul says in 1 Cor. 15; 41 that
"one star differeth from another star in glory". So this choir is
verily a symphony, a harmonious consonance of all the single
individualities, all of whom He calls "by name".

And finally the stars are mentioned once more in Psalm 148; 3,
in the grand Halleluja of the universe. Just as in Psalm 136 the
words of the eternally enduring mercy are added to each sentence,
so Psalm 148 contains the ever-repeated exhortation to join in the
great chorus of praise. It begins with the heavens and the higher
worlds, passes on to angels and heavenly hosts, and only with the
sun, moon and stars passes over from the invisible into visibility.
"Praise him, sun and moon, praise him all ye stars of the night."

These three passages supplement one another. In Psalm 136 the
stars come forth from the merciful self-communication and revelation of the eternal Godhead. In Psalm 147 the stars appear as
multiplicity and yet unity, a symphony of individualities. In Psalm
148 the stars are clear mirrors which radiate back to the Creator
His splendour, in that they "praise" Him. This is like a reversal
of Psalm 136. These three passages which refer to the relation
of God to the stars and of the stars to God, contrast with our
Psalm 8 where the relation is shown between the stars and man.
"When I consider thy heavens . . . moon and stars." One must
pause a while and feel the quietness of contemplation, how every-

thing sinks away around us, and only the starry heaven remains, which in the land of the Psalmist shines with brilliant clarity and radiance. Let us feel for a while the calm peace—all self forgotten —of this contemplation, "when I consider thy heavens . . . moon and stars . . .".

But now this forgetfulness of self issues into the question about man. A deep inner logic lies in the fact that this experience of the stars, which carries us out into the infinite universe, turns back to man. A deep contemplation of the stars does not imply getting lost in the far spaces, but coming in connection with the eternal powers who work together from the periphery into the centre, in order to bring forth man. We sense in the stars the cosmic dwelling-places of the higher beings who take part in our human evolution. The macrocosm without stands in intimate relation with the microcosm, man. This is the inner logic of the transition from the contemplation of the stars to the question about the human being. Again we observe the upward and downward movement between heaven and earth, peculiar to the 8th Psalm.

What is man that thou art mindful of him?

One must not hear this question with the ears of the modern "enlightened" men of natural science. For them it would mean: "What indeed is the speck of dust, man, in face of these giant astronomical dimensions!" What indeed can man signify in the universe? Less than nothing. To consider the world from the point of view of material size is far from the mood of the Psalm. Incidentally, this "speck-of-dust mood" has no doubt the appearance of praiseworthy humility; it is, however, very convenient. Through a purely quantitative view one reduces man to nothingness, and then in light-hearted irresponsibility one can lead a morally inferior life. If the starry heaven is understood again as the revelation of creative spirit-powers, then the question: "What is man?" is raised once more in all earnestness.

The being whom we call man is not yet completed. Called to grow in the image of God, he is still in process of becoming. For the sake of his evolution to this distant goal he goes through a "history". An integral part of this history is the Fall of Man presented in the Old Testament in hieroglyphic visionary pictures. This event severed man from the world of his origin, and enabled the powers of death to draw near him. There is an echo of this in the text of our Psalm, where for "man" the usual "adam" is not used at first, but the word *enosch*. This denotes "the transitory", "the perishable". Somewhat as we speak of men as "mortals". Thus: "What is a mortal that thou art mindful of him, that thou bearest him in thy divine consciousness?" In the next lines, however, the word "Adam" appears in *ben-adam* which denotes "son of man".

And the son of man that thou takest care of him?

Man is absorbed in the contemplation of the starry heavens. This could not happen if he were made only of what is transitory. Beholding the stars man becomes conscious of the riddle of death, which has been added to his nature: "What is mortal man that thou cherishest him in thy thoughts?" Then the gaze passes from the man of to-day into the future. "The son of man." Again "Adam" is used in the Hebrew, which stresses the relation to the earth, but without implying material transitoriness. The "son" of man—this is the human being growing into the future, striving towards new possibilities. It is the figure which, out of the old Adam marked by Death and the Fall, is to come forth one day as something new. In the New Testament "son of man" appears significantly as characterizing Christ; for He alone can overcome the powers of the Fall and make the human being capable of a divine future.

Note too the polarity of the elements of thought and will in the words "mindful of" and "takest care of". God is mindful of mortal man, He carries him in His consciousness. He cares for, takes charge of, the son of man. He lets His vigorous help stream to him. The Hebrew word is sometimes also rendered by "visit" (*visitare*) in the positive sense of going as a visitor. The Godhead unites itself with the future form of man and inclines to him with strength of being. Here the mysteries of Christ are touched upon from afar, as in premonition. Only in the light of Christ does the question of man and his future find its answer. Only, too, in the light of Christ as the one who will reinstate and perfect true manhood, do the following verses, speaking of man's glory and honour, receive their full meaning.

Before we pass on to these, let us look back once more and see how man meets us in three forms, how in Psalm 8 he bears the three names: the child—the mortal—the son of man. The "child" is the human being still fully enveloped in the divine forces of his origin. The "mortal" is the grown man of the Fall, who has bought his consciousness at the cost of being permeated with the powers of death. The "son of man" stands as the figure of the future in the glory of Christ.

That the Psalm does not answer the question which arose from contemplation of the stars, in the sense of man as a grain of dust, is shown in the way it continues. The glory of his origin and the glory of future perfection lie in these words:

> Thou hast made him almost a God,
> Crowning him with the light of revelation
> and splendour of majesty.

Man—"almost a God". In this "almost" lies the drama of his evolution, his problem. He feels himself called to divine status. Lucifer knew how to lay hold of him through this noble urge for perfection. "Ye shall be as gods". But only Another will really redeem this promise—"ye are Gods" (John 10; 34).

The radiating crown on the head was an accepted image in ancient times, indicating that man was not "closed" above, but reaching upwards into the divine light. This man is spiritually crowned with "glory and majesty", with *Kābôd* and *Hadar*. The former word often stands in the Old Testament for the aura of the Godhead when the tabernacle, or later the temple, is filled with the shining traces of its presence. The second word means "radiating sublimity"—majesty. Certain early Rabbis saw in this crowning with *Kābôd* and *Hadar* a reference to the endowment of man with the "higher soul" (the *neschamah aljonah* in the works of Kimchi and Salomon ben Melech); and rightly so. This mysterious event finds its full consummation again only through the Christ. The Book of Revelation speaks of the "Crown of Life" which is given to him who goes with Christ through death, and the warning is uttered "that no one take thy crown". For the adversary would snatch from man his higher spirituality and thrust him down into animal nature.

The Psalm, which in the image of the crown of light looked up to the heights, now turns once more towards the earth. After having considered that which is above man and which descends as a crown upon his head, it passes on to what is beneath him:

> Thou hast set him to rule over the works of thy hands;
> Thou hast put all things under his feet . . .

The created world is put in subjection to him who is crowned with spirit. Man participates in both worlds. Upwards he extends to the Godhead, downwards he shares in the creature through his body. Mediating between the visible and invisible world, he is called to be the representative of God—the *Vicarius Dei*—on earth. Should he permit the opposing powers to rob him of his crown, he becomes a tyrant, an exploiter of the earth. That he should subdue the earth is a divine commission (Gen 1; 28). But he dare not forget that he may only rule the earth as bearer of the spirit crown, and that the world beneath him is "the work of thy hands". Herein lies the whole programme for human work and civilization on the earth.

And now the animal world is especially mentioned as subjected to man, not in the order of Creation as in Genesis, but in the reverse order. The text begins with the higher animals, those nearer to the human being, and then advances to those further removed, the creatures of air and water. First the domestic animals, then the wild animals (beasts of the field), then birds and finally fishes.

> All sheep and oxen, yea and the beasts of the field;
> The fowl of the air and the fish of the sea and
> whatsoever travels by the paths of the seas.

This rulership of man over the beasts has another aspect, a more inward one. There exists something like an underground connection between the animals and the various impulses of man's soul. Fairy-tales and dreams make known to us in manifold ways that the animal world represents the totality of man's emotional nature. Certain soul-forces are objectified in the animal forms; they dwell also within the soul. To rule over the animal, including the animal in one's own inner being, through a connection with the higher realm of Spirit, is the task which lies before man. He stands between angel and beast. In Psalm 91 this finds classic expression: "For he shall give his angels charge over thee . . . they shall bear thee up in their hands . . . thou shalt tread upon the lion and the adder, the young lion and the dragon shalt thou trample under feet" (91; 11–13). Not in the proud "Luciferic" sense is the majesty of man intended here.

The Psalm concludes with the same sentence with which it began:

> O Lord, our Lord,
> How gloriously is the splendour of thy Name
> reflected in all the earth!

The same sentence as at the beginning. But it has grown richer. Man has been built into this song of praise. When man's dignity is fully established the Name of God can truly reveal itself on earth. Dedication to being human is man's true Divine Service.

God in Nature

PSALM 104

The 104th Psalm is like an echo in human form of the story of Creation in Genesis; the events recorded in the succession of the days of Creation resound in the Psalm, which is composed in seven sections.

I

THE HEAVENS

Praise the Lord, O my Soul. O Lord my God, thou art very great.

This expression "very great" is more than a merely edifying turn of expression. It holds the key to an understanding of the creation of the world. "Great", for ancient times, is a term for a spirituality of such overflowing force that it can pour itself creatively into an outer world. A spirituality which from inner abundance can become "spiritual-physical". The pre-eminence of the purely spiritual as the original beginning is not infringed, but we must think of a Spirit capable of creating a world.

The 104th Psalm traces the path that leads from the essential being, the inner existence of God, to the becoming of the world. In this progress several stages may be distinguished. It begins with the "spiritual-physical" quality of the state of "greatness". What then proceeds out of this quality of the Godhead is designated by words that in the original Hebrew text have a mantric power: *"hod we hadar"*.

Thou hast clothed thyself in radiance-of-being
and splendour of majesty.

"Radiance-of-being and splendour-of-majesty"—the meaning,
but not the spoken sound of the two words may perhaps be thus
distantly reproduced. They are unusually impressive, both in con-
sonants and vowels, and particularly in their sequence. The first
word *hod* appears in the Greek translation of the Septuagint as
exomologesis, Latin "confessio" and English "confession". This
would suggest that in the confession, the acknowledgment, something inward is turned outwards and made manifest. Goethe
called his works "Fragments of a great Confession".

The two words express a streaming out from the unmanifested
into the manifested. There is as yet nothing externally physical,
we are still in a region of etheric light. Only in what follows do
we enter the realm of the visible world, even though "light" is
not actually "visible", but only renders the world visible for us.
However, compared with *hod* and *hadar*, light is a step further
into external existence.

Thou coverest thyself with light as with a garment.
Thou stretchest out the heavens like a tent.
Thou buildest thy high house in the waters.

Only now we have reached the "Let there be light" of Genesis. The radiance-of-being and splendour-of-majesty belongs to
a still earlier, preceding stage. Now the heavens appear together
with the light. Then "the waters". As yet this is no earthly water,
nor is it water existing in cloud-form, but it is the "water above
the firmament", a heavenly ocean of etheric fluid forces.

Let us look again at this succession. Being Great—Radiance of
Being—Splendour of Majesty—Light—Waters. It is the path
into ever denser forms of existence, the path from within to without. This becomes very evident when we set the other series
beside it; the words of comparison which express the relation to
the Godhead: garment, mantle, tent, high-palace (balcony, upper
chamber). The "garment" lies closest—and the Psalm compares

with it the radiation which precedes the light. The "mantle" is a degree more "external". Removed still further from the original Person is the "tent", which however is not so far removed from the "mantle" as, finally, the "house". With the "Being Great" at the beginning we are still within the very person of God. Then begins the manifestation, and the resulting world detaches itself more and more from the immediacy of the Creator, it covers Him, concealing-manifesting, manifesting-concealing as garment, as mantle, as tent, as house. But this house of the heavens is at the same time the temple of His direct presence.

From this high "Light-heaven" we now descend to the atmospheric heaven which is nearer to earth. We pass over at the same time from a world of tranquil being and tranquil radiance into the dynamic spheres of active forces.

> Thou makest the clouds thy chariot.
> Thou stormest forth upon the wings of the wind.
> Thou lettest thine angels work in winds,
> Thy lofty ministers in flaming fire.

Clouds and winds bear the Lord in His movement, when He forsakes the Temple of His heavenly calm, and "goes out of Himself", "fares forth" in the ecstasy of the storm. Finally, contemplation passes from the divine Person Himself to the forces which have detached themselves from Him, as independent spirit-personalities. These are the "messengers", the "angels" (*angeloi*) which can incorporate themselves in the wafting winds. There are the "lofty ministers" of God, his "*liturgoi*" as the Greek translation says, who can embody themselves in the flaming fire, in lightning. The Hebrew word *meshoreth* does not mean a slavish servant, but one who from free will serves as "Minister", as server in the highest sense. The ninefold order of the heavenly hierarchies has as the lowest degree the messengers, the angels. They can incorporate in the wafting winds. The highest hierarchy is the "Seraphim" which means the "Burning Ones". They reveal themselves in the fire of lightning. The Prophet

Isaiah sees them in his great Temple Vision as the heavenly cele-
brants who begin to sound the hymn of the "Thrice Holy", the
"Sanctus".

II

THE EARTH

Through the elemental spheres of clouds, storms and lightning,
we descend to the solid earth.

> *He has laid the foundations of the earth that*
> *it should not be shaken for ever.*

In order to characterize in its stages the gradual detachment
of the world from the Creator, Rudolf Steiner used a series of
four concepts: Being—Manifestation—Activity—Finished Work.
"Thou art great"—here we are still in the Being. With the Light-
heaven, the Manifestation began to issue from the Being, but it
still remained intimately linked with it. The world of clouds and
winds, of lightning and thunderstorms—this was the sphere of
Activity, where the Being is represented by the forces sent out
but Himself remains still further in the background. With the
solid earth the stage of the Finished Work is reached; it is accomplished, finished, released, henceforth set free from the Creator.
The end product is as congealed lava.

In its stony hardness the earth has an important function in the
evolution of man. Man is to come to independence. To this end
he must be withdrawn for a time from the direct life of divine
being, in order to become aware of his own power of initiative
in a world of death. It is precisely in the rigid element of earth,
isolated from the immediate life of the higher worlds, that man
can awaken to consciousness of himself as an individual personality. Moreover the solid earth holds fast the works of man and
sets impressively before his eyes the results of his deeds, whether
they have been constructive or destructive.

The production of this solid earth was a particular work of the ego-creating God.

> *Thou coveredst it with the deep as with a garment.*
> *The waters stood above the mountains.*
> *At thy rebuke they fled;*
> *At the voice of thy thunder they hasted away.*

The Deep, *thehom*, appears often in the Old Testament as a sinister demonic being, as a kind of dragon of the pre-world chaos. The evolution of the firm earth with its solid ground for the developing of man's self-dependence was seen as a God-willed design. In the ever-recurring floods the "dragons", the luciferic beings, who were servants of chaos, were active. In the Babylonian myth, Marduk, the Babylonian Michael, subdues Tiamat, the dragon of the primeval world. So here, the ego-creating God "rebukes" with a voice of thunder the powers of chaos and frees the earthly scene for man's activity. And now at length the earth emerges from the primeval waters.

> *There went forth the mountains, there sank down*
>   *the valleys,*
> *Unto the place which thou hast founded for them.*
> *Thou hast set a bound that they (the waters) may*
>   *not pass over,*
> *That they turn not again to cover the earth.*

The 95th Psalm says still more plainly how the surface of the Earth is shaped by God: "And thy hands have formed the dry land" (95; 5). (In the Greek *eplasan*.) Thus mountains and valleys are the scene prepared by divine Providence for the unfolding of man's destiny. We remember many sacred mountains upon which men received divine revelation, and think of the deep Jordan valley, lying far below sea-level, where at the Baptism by John, God entered into existence on earth.

III

THE LIFE OF THE EARTH

A boundary is set to the flood. The continents are there in order
to give continuity and conciseness to earthly human consciousness. In the solid element the earth is for the first time truly
"Earth". But if the earth consisted only of earth it would become a wilderness of death. Lucifer worked in the floods of
chaos. In the hardened earth the Lord of Death appears, "Ahriman", as the Persians called him. The earth must be kept living.
The water-element, no longer as *Thehom*, the Dragon of the
primeval deep, but now as a servant helps the earth to maintain
life.

Without water no plants. Water is the necessary "medium"
of life, the vehicle of the "etheric" life-forces, which cannot
approach the hard crust of the earth directly but which can be
active in the liquid.

No life upon earth without water. And just as the moulding
of the earth in hill and dale is no accident but the work of the
divine "potter", so too are the streams and rivers in the landscape, which well up from the springs, the result of organizing
divine action.

> *Thou who sendest the springs into the valleys,*
> *Which run among the hills.*
> *They give drink to every beast of the field,*
> *The wild beast quenches his thirst.*
> *By them the fowls of the air have their habitation*
> *Which sing among the branches.*

Many commentaries have pointed out the poetic beauty of this
description. The vivifying water not only appears in brooks and
streams. It also falls upon the earth as rain. By falling in drops the
water is prevented from being destructive and is wonderfully
suited to the needs of the plants. Moreover in ascending and

evaporating, water has been enriched with certain forces which it now brings down with it in the rain as a blessing. The ancients rightly believed that something came with it from God. Its "etheric" quality is a gift from heavenly spheres. It is a "blessing" from "above".

> *Thou waterest the hills from thy heavenly house*
> *Thou satisfiest the land with the fruits thou createst.*

Then the Psalm describes in detail the fruitfulness of the earth:

> *Thou causest the grass to grow for the cattle*
> *And grain for the service of man,*
> *That he may bring forth bread out of the earth.*

Cattle can eat the grass as it grows. But grain must be worked for, so that it can serve man. Human effort must be added to the natural process in order to cultivate the grain and bake bread. The production of corn for bread—*agricultura*—is the origin of "culture", and also of "cult". Both words are derived from the word "*colere*", to till the soil. Here, in connection with the preparation of bread, man is mentioned for the first time in Psalm 104.

> *That the wine make glad the heart of man,*
> *That his face may shine with oil,*
> *And that bread may strengthen man's heart.*

The trinity, wine—oil—bread, points also to the sphere of worship. Bread and wine are both brought into connection with the human heart. The bread "establishes our heart in steadfastness", the wine makes it "glad". In the service of Christ, these two become His body and His blood.

In addition to bread and wine with their relation to the heart oil is mentioned, which is likewise a sacramental substance. "That his countenance may shine with oil." Oil is related to light. It is used in the Anointing Service and in the Consecration of Priests as the agent of a spiritualizing process. It is not connected with the heart, but with the countenance in which man's spirit-nature is revealed.

The Psalm then passes from the cultivated plants to nature in the wild. Linking up again to the words, "He watereth the hills from above" it now reads:

> The trees of the Lord are full of sap; the cedars
> of Lebanon which he hath planted: where the
> birds make their nests. The stork has her nest on
> the tree top. The high hills are the realm of the
> wild goats and the rocks are a refuge for the
> conies.

The manner in which the "trees of Jehovah" are spoken of here, the cedars of Lebanon which He himself planted, is magnificent. Primeval forests stood on Lebanon, nature untouched by man. Time and again the Old Testament witnesses to the wonder and awe with which those mighty cedar trees were observed. The presence of God Himself was felt in the midst of such forests. (Psalm 80; 11 also speaks of the "cedars of God".) When one considers the peculiar lack of sense for natural beauty in later Jewry, one is glad to hear such tones in the Old Testament. In the stories of the Patriarch Abraham sacred groves and the planting of sacred trees play an important part. But the cedars of Lebanon were felt as if planted by God himself.

If we would transpose the "conies" into our European high mountain world we could perhaps think of the marmot. Wandering over a lonely hillside set with boulders one can hear the call of the marmot that warns of the approach of man. The world in which one hears the call of the marmot and the clattering of the stones which have become detached under the foot of the fleeing chamois—that is a world of untouched solitude, far from man and his civilization. In the Psalm's devotional contemplation of Nature this world remote from man is also included. It is as though the psalmist felt that the sphere of human activity required around it a zone of undisturbed nature belonging to God.

IV

SUN AND MOON

In the account given in Genesis, the celestial bodies, sun, moon and stars only became visible on the fourth Day of Creation, even though the "light-heaven" had been there for some time. Similarly Psalm 104, following the events of Genesis in a freer manner, comes to speak of stars, moon and sun in its fourth section.

The Psalm began with a descent out of the spheres of light to the waters of heaven and the clouds, and then down to the firm earth. In considering the earth, this way was reversed: first the earth as "solid land", then the earth in so far as it is kept living by water. And now the earth is described with the great variety of emotions of which its inhabitants are capable, and which form an "astral" relation with the celestial lights. For sun and moon do not appear here "on their own", but in their relation to soul life on earth. The stars, the *astra*, influence "astrality" on the earth.

> *He appointed the moon for seasons (to give signs),*
> *The sun knoweth his going down.*
> *Thou makest darkness and it is night,*
> *Wherein all the beasts of the forest do creep forth.*
> *The young lions roar after their prey,*
> *This is their prayer to God for meat.*
> *The sun ariseth, they gather themselves together*
> *And lay them down in their dens.*
> *Man goeth forth unto his work*
> *And to his labours until the evening.*

First, the moon. The moon stands in the evening sky as a "sign". It marks the divisions of time, according to its phases. The significance of the lunar cycles is far-reaching for life on earth. Even the date of the Passover is fixed by these cycles (and the Christian Easter). The sun "knoweth his going down". It "knows" that earthly creatures may not be uninterruptedly exposed to its effects. So in going down it makes place for the kingdom of night, ruled by the moon.

"Darkness" and "night", as in Genesis, have essential being. They are not merely "absence of light". With the night the "astral" world of the moon comes to life, to which the animals belong. Moon-"astrality", not yet penetrated by ego-consciousness, under the spell of dreams, makes the beasts of prey stir in the dark forests, makes the lions roar. The roaring, the cries, the bellowings of the beasts by night arouse a weird feeling in us of the remoteness from man of this animal soul-world dating from the world's primeval ages.

It has been thought touchingly naïve that the Psalm implies a prayer to God in the roaring of lions. But in general the naïve view stands mostly nearer to the original fact. The stirring of the animal souls is still close to the divine worlds. These original instincts are no longer so innocent in man as in the beast, but are poisoned through the contact with an egotistic selfhood which has not yet achieved a selfless Ego. Among men this direct proximity to God has been almost entirely lost.

The moon-world is overcome by the rising of the Sun. The nocturnal beasts of prey hide in their holes. In the soul life of man something similar occurs. Nightmares, bad dreams, anxiety, spectres—all this vanishes when the sun comes up. It helps man to kindle spirit-consciousness in his ego, it brings him to himself, helps him to be himself. In a mood of festive ritual it is said: "Man goeth forth unto his work". It is the sunlit day with which the human being is most deeply united. His work belongs to the light of day, his "labour until the evening".

The fourth section closes with this archetypal picture of the worker who "works so long as it is day". The contemplation of the earthly world has reached its climax. At first it is simply hard ground; then enlivened by water and adorned by plants; then the souls of the beasts begin to stir; and finally man, related to the sun, goes about his work on earth. Here the Psalm rises to words of wonder:

> O Lord, how manifold are thy works!
> In wisdom hast thou made them all.
> The Earth is filled with what is thine.

Literally, the Earth is full of thy possessions. God, the Creator, has laid something of His own into the earthly world.

V

THE SEA

Just as Genesis makes the swarming animal life in the sea (fifth day) follow upon the appearance of the celestial lights (on the fourth day) so too does Psalm 104 turn once more to the sea and its living creatures.

> So is this great and wide sea,
> Wherein are things creeping innumerable,
> Both small and great beasts.
> There the sea-wonders take their way;
> Leviathan whom thou hast made to play with thee.

Here Thehom, the primeval flood, still lives, but within the bounds given to it. The sea is like a memory of primeval stages before the earth had hardened into solid form. Indeed, everything alive has had its beginning in the sea. The composition of our human blood shows a mysterious relationship with sea-water —memory of far-distant stages of the development of our bodily nature.

In his "Classical Walpurgis Night" Goethe takes Homunculus, who would fain originate from a true bodily nature, to the sea. Proteus, the master of transformation, advises him: "Thou must commence in the wide ocean yonder!" And Thales, the Sage, who taught that everything originally began in water, says: "Yield to the worthy exhortation from the first step to start creation; for prompt activity prepare. Thou'lt move by external norms, through thousand and yet thousand forms, and ere thou'rt man there's time to spare."

According to an illuminating conjecture it should not read "there go the ships" but instead of ships: "sea-monsters". The leviathan is then mentioned directly in connection with this. The mythical sea-dragon is an echo of long-banished worlds of the saurians. "To play with him."—The "play" points to artistic activity. In all the changes of form among the living and en-souled plasma, divine formative force is at work—comes into play. It is "in play" on the infinite possibilities of form in organic substance, until after this great prelude the human form finally appears. The fantastic prehistoric shapes, sea-monsters and dragons lie, too, on the way to the final human form.

VI

THE MYSTERY OF SUSTAINING THE WORLD

These wait all upon thee; that thou mayst give
them their meat in due season.
That thou givest them, they gather;
Thou openest thy hand, they are filled with good.
Thou hidest thy face, they are troubled:
Thou takest away their Breath, they die, and
return to their dust.
Thou sendest forth thy Breath—they are created
And thou renewest the face of the earth.

In a sweeping glance at the totality of living creatures, God is acknowledged and honoured. Three pictures express what God continuously means for the world, even after creation has come to an end: the opening hand, the face turned towards or away, the ingoing and outgoing breath. These pictures harmonize into a wonderfully organic trinity. (They are known in Anthroposophy as the "nerves and senses" system, the "rhythmic" system working in pulse and breath, and the "metabolism and limbs" system.)

In the head and countenance where our principal senses operate, our consciousness is awake. The basic condition for the existence of the world is that God turns His face towards it. If He should turn His face away, the fear of annihilation comes over all living beings. The world remains in existence as long as it is beheld and affirmed by the divine consciousness.

Breath lives in the rhythmic sphere. The world exists so long as the divine breath permeates it. If God draws in His breath, it falls into nothingness. Similarly in Job (34; 14, 15), "If he gather unto himself his spirit and his breath, all flesh shall perish together". This view is reminiscent of ancient Indian wisdom. The world is dependent on the breath of God. He breathes out: worlds arise. He breathes in: worlds perish. And so it goes on in exalted rhythms, incalculably long. Manvantaras and Pralayas, Cosmic Days and Cosmic Nights, are the result of this divine rhythmic breath. In the creating exhalation the breath of life (the Hebrew *ruach* is both "spirit" and "breath") is still directly God's —"thy Breath". When God withdraws the breath, it is observed that meanwhile it has become the individualized breath of separate beings; for it now reads: "their" breath. "Thou takest away their breath." The life of God becomes the life of the individual beings. But inasmuch as He takes back the world into Himself, "their" breath returns to its source.

To close or open a hand is a voluntary movement. The divine hand opens, the beings are filled with "good". "Good" is a word that ultimately belongs to God alone. God gives away of His own being, His own substance, so that something can come into existence. Nothing would be there, if this mystery of divine self-imparting, self-surrender did not exist. The whole world is fed from divine substance. The reception of nourishment is again only a picture, an image. Even without actual eating, a being "lives" from the Godhead in every moment of its mere existing. Apart from the taking of nourishment, there is the great communion of all creatures in the Substance of God Himself. "Thou openest thy hand—they are filled with good." "Good" in the original text is the same word as "goodness". In a wider sense every good thing, all goods, even the everyday consumer goods are dependant on the divine self-imparting, the original goodness. This mystery is acted out in the Last Supper. The opening hand is the gesture of the great divine "Take this". (Psalm 145; 16, offers a parallel to this: "Thou openest thy hand and satisfiest the desire of every living thing".)

From different aspects the relationship of God to His world is set forth in these three pictures. In order that the world may be, God must turn His face to it, He must breathe into it His breath, He must open his hand and distribute.

The face of the earth is renewed. The earth has already passed through manifold forms; there was once the earth of the coal-forests and the saurians. Each time the face of the earth was uniform, formed according to a definite "style". These ancient worlds passed away when their hour had struck and gave place to new epochs. The surface of the earth has thus already been many times renewed. This is true too for the succession of civilizations. All these events are associated with the taking in and giving out of breath by God. The world is not only "sustained"; in greater or smaller rhythms it is continuously renewed by the living breath of the Spirit, which ever and again sends out new waves of becoming, as "Creator Spiritus".

VII

CLOSING VERSES

The glory of the Lord shall endure for ever:
The Lord shall rejoice in his works.
He looketh on the earth and it trembleth,
He toucheth the hills and they smoke,

I will sing unto the Lord as long as I live;
I will sing praise to my God while I have my being.
My meditation of him shall be sweet,
I will be glad in the Lord.
Let the sinners be consumed out of the earth,
And let the wicked be no more!
Bless thou the Lord, O my Soul.
Praise ye the Lord.

The closing lines admit that there is also dissonance in the symphony of creation. The wonderful symphony is disturbed through the evil in man. The psalmist knows of no other solution than to desire that the evil-doers be exterminated from the earth.

The Fall of Man follows the creation of the world. Since the song of praise is honest and realistic it cannot pass over this fact. It calls for a sentence of punishment in order that the creation may be purified and re-established. The Mystery of Redemption through Christ has not yet been revealed. Nor can it yet be evident that the permitting of evil was only a withdrawal, preceding a new creation which was to go beyond nature. Man was set upon his evolutionary path, in order that, as one who has himself been redeemed, he may in future times place his independence freely into the service of the divine.

But this dark shadow, this unresolved discord cannot really disturb the impression that the 104th Psalm is altogether a great hymn of joy. Joy and gladness is the real character of this song of praise. In the final verses this is said in so many words. God rejoices in His work. Without joy no creation. In response comes the rejoicing of man in God. The sight of nature and its beauty turns into joy in God: "I will be glad in the Lord".

The Psalm ends as it began, with the exhortation to one's own soul to join in the song of praise.

The Heavens Declare

PSALM 19

I

THE STARRY HEAVENS

The 19th Psalm opens in a mood of marvelling contemplation of the starry sky. Its first words are "the heavens" and the whole Psalm is dedicated to this subject and pours forth from it. Whilst the Psalmist remains absorbed in selfless contemplation of the shining worlds they begin to sound and speak to his inner ear. "The heavens declare the glory of God and the firmament proclaimeth His handiwork".

For the ancient world the "music of the spheres" was a definite supersensible experience. The heavens not only shine: to the opened spiritual ear they sound, ring, finally even speak. There is an echo of this in the opening words of Goethe's Faust:

> The sun-orb sings in emulation,
> Mid brother spheres his ancient round.

The heavens "declare"—the Hebrew word is of the same origin as the word *sepher*, the "book"; the book in which things are entered, enumerated, declared, "booked". The starry heavens are the archetypal book, the book of books. The heavens were the first holy script. The "Holy Scripture" is a mirror, an image of this. Even to-day Bible and Ritual Book on the altar represent the Book of the Heavens.

The content of this cosmic proclamation is the "Glory of God".

"Glory" is, however, too superficial a rendering. It is the splendour of revelation to which the Psalm refers.

If the first sentence speaks of the divine revelation in the splendour of light, the second sentence refers to the divine power: "And the firmament proclaimeth his handiwork". The firmament (*firmus* means fixed) is for modern man an out-of-date scientific concept. To the scientist of today the tranquillity of the firmament is an illusion; space for him is full of movement and tensions. And yet the ancient word "firmament" is somehow true. It conveys to us the spiritual experience of a divine world, resting deeply in itself despite all creative activity—a world eternally founded in its own being. This spiritual experience was released through the sight of the stars. It is not for nothing that the fixed stars in their stability appear to the human eye as resting in their places. It is just as little accidental as the blue of the sky, which indeed is also "only" an optical phenomenon. The pictures in which the universe offers itself to the eye of man are not merely accidental. They have their own picture-value, their own realistic justification, upon quite a different plane from their purely physical existence. As pictures which the cosmic artist has allowed to appear thus and not otherwise before the eyes of man, they have their own laws independent of the purely physical nature and condition. To this extent it is justified if we contemplate the firmament, to feel face to face with a world of immovable calm, eternally founded upon itself, one which fills us with inner stability and assurance and harmony.

The Psalm touches the roots of eternity. It rests at first in the contemplation of the highest spheres. Then it gradually descends. It is as though it traverses at the same time the path of incarnation, by which the super-earthly betakes itself down to earth to become flesh. From the eternal world of the immovable stars we descend gradually into the sphere of time. We have not yet reached the spatial and corporeal. But the soul which was surrendered to the timeless and eternal, surrounds itself now with the fine web of the *temporal*. Before it enters the spatial body it assumes, as it were, the time-body as a fine sheath:

Day unto day uttereth speech
and night unto night showeth knowledge.

We have entered the world of rhythmical time. This is shown impressively in the original text, "*jom le jom . . . lajelah le lajelah*", "day unto day . . . night unto night". Quite literally, it reads, "Day lets word arise to day, night makes knowledge living to night". Here a fine differentiation is made between day and night. The day brings to light the "manifestation", it proclaims the word, it brings it "to the light of day". But this "bringing to light" is only one side of the process of learning to know. When we sleep, mysteriously in the depths of the soul all that we have acquired by conscious experience by day is further worked upon throughout the night. Everyone is aware how a thought can live and develop further when we "sleep on it". What the day makes evident to us is permeated by higher life in the night. Life is added to Light. In Hebrew, *jom* is masculine, *lajelah* is feminine. In the clear concept of the day a male element is active, as it were; the night, however, is a mother of life.

Only now does the Psalm reach our earth and its spatial, material existence. But it does not see the earth with ordinary, everyday sight; descending from heaven, it hears the word of the stars resounding in the corporeal element. The terrestrial shows itself to be ordered, fashioned, "sounded through" by the celestial.

Their line has gone out through all the earth.

This "line" is the measuring line, the "tape measure". Inasmuch as the chaos of earthly substances comes to life in manifold forms, our enlightened eye now beholds the heavenly forces at work "measuring", setting a standard. Just as in the well-known experiment of the chladnic figures, iron filings on a glass plate take on forms from resounding tones, the sound-figures of the stars work into formations on the earth.

There is no speech nor language where their voice is not heard.
Their line goes into all lands ("erez" is at the same time "the
    earth")
and their words to the end of the world.

We can now review the first part of the Psalm. It leads us through three worlds. First, the eternal in eternity. The fixed stars radiating in the firmament. Then, the eternal entering into time. The temporal, rhythmic world of day and night stands as mediator between the eternal light of heaven and the darkness of the earth. Finally, the eternal working into space, the working of the stars in earthly substances, the sound-figures of the celestial spheres in the dust of the earth:

> *The celestial spheres declare the light-manifestation*
> *   of the eternal,*
> *The firmament extolleth the work of his hands.*
> *Day unto day uttereth the word of revelation,*
> *Night unto night bringeth knowledge to life.*
> *Not inaudible are these words and this speaking;*
> *Their sounding brings order into all earth-existence.*
> *To the ends of the earth's circuit their speaking*
> *   resounds and is mighty.*

II

THE SUN

The first part of the Psalm has led us down the path from the heights of the stars into the depths of matter. When we find ourselves again in earthly existence the splendour of the stars grows pale. We hear it still echoing in earthly substances. Then all this vanishes before the glow of sunrise. The deeper foundations of existence are concealed behind the veil of the senses. The rising sun deprives us of the sight of the stars but it shows us instead the earth as the field of our labours, the scene of our actual life as man.

> *Which cometh as a bridegroom out of his chamber,*
> *and rejoiceth as a hero to run his race.*

His going forth is from the end of the heaven
And his circuit unto the ends of it,
And there is nothing hid from the heat thereof.

In Hebrew as well as in English the sun is masculine. It is en-souled by a "sun-spirit", the "sun genius". Here in the Psalm it becomes a manifestation of the Son, while behind the stars the Father-God appears as the eternal Ground of the World.

People of ancient times did not yet possess the fixed indepen-dent ego-consciousness which we have today. They were depen-dent on the sun for coming to their aid. They were only truly themselves in the shining of the sun. With the going down of the sun the border lines of their personal consciousness became in-distinct, and with the dimming of the "ego" the supersensible—the divine but also the demonic—came towards them. The further humanity receded from its divine origin, the more night became the realm of spectres and ghosts, instead of being the "holy night" of revelation. In Christ the Godhead appeared as the great I AM in the bright day-consciousness, in order to sanctify the awakened human ego and to unite it again with the Divine World. In pre-Christian times something like a promise of Christ shone down to man out of the sun. Even to-day we still feel how the sunrise can rescue us from the horror of an uneasy night and make a "new man" of us. The sun gives fresh vital energy, new joy and a "holy soberness". It drives away the phantoms of the night.

The Psalm depicts the lofty Sun-Spirit in two images: as Hero and as Bridegroom. The Hero is the outstanding man who shows others what it really means to be man; pursuing a path, complet-ing a course. The stronger the personality, the more strongly marked is the line of this course. Many a man idles away his time straying to the right and left of his path like Little Red Riding Hood when she meets the wolf. The higher the human being reaches, the more he is a "Hero", so much the more does a cer-tain line and significant form appear in his life. In the Ancient Mysteries a particular grade of initiation was called "Sun Hero"

—literally, *Heliodromos*, who like the sun runs his course sure of his goal and full of strength. Thus St. Paul could say in old age, "I have finished the course" (*ton dromon teteleka*—2 Tim. 4; 7). In its sublime, unswerving path the sun daily displays the image of a glorious "course". In the *Commentary on the Psalms* by Professor R. Kittel, there is a beautiful description of how the Israelites experienced this daily course of the sun: "Behind the eastern mountains, the ranges of Moab or Bashan, and further back behind the infinite eastern desert, the sun rises for the inhabitants of Palestine from the scented mist of the horizon in red and golden brilliant splendour, of which western man can hardly form a conception. It moves along in its majestic course over the land, to dip down once more in the evening into the blue waves of the western sea, behind the cliffs of Joppa or on the dunes at the foot of Carmel, again and again in red-gold haze wrapt as in a purple mantle".

The course of a Hero reaching his goal was a prophecy of the earthly path of Christ. The Gospel of St. Mark, in particular, describes the life of Christ on earth as unswerving—a sun-path that must take this course and no other. Again and again one finds in Mark, "And straightway . . . And straightway . . ." (an exact rendering of the Greek word *euthys*"). The "straightway" which appears so often in Mark has no hint of haste or breathlessness. It indicates that all the deeds of Christ lie on the direct path of his course as a Sun-Hero.

But Christ is not only the great example of a runner on the path, he is more: he is the archetype of our true being working creatively within us. The arechetypal plant does not stay outside the plant but is present in it, concretely active and creative. So does the Christ desire to draw into us and work within us as creative archetype. At this stage our relation to him passes over into mysticism: he is the Bridegroom. This word echoes from the Mysteries. John the Baptist "rejoices over the Bridegroom's voice" and Christ frequently describes himself as the "Bridegroom". The Sun-Spirit is called the Bridegroom because he is to receive the full surrender of the human soul, with which he will unite himself in the innermost communion of the "Mystic Marriage". If we follow Kittel, the Hebrew text in the next line is somewhat uncertain. If one single letter is altered, it would read "A tent is pitched for the sun in the ocean". This sounds like an echo from ancient myths. Men saw the sun in the evening dip down into the sea and thus arose the mythological picture of the bridal chamber of the sun-god in the depths of the ocean. A higher truth is revealed in this image. The depths of the ocean become a genuine allegory for the depths of the soul. The Christ who is experienced in bright day-consciousness unites at night with deeper regions of the soul's life. The ancient mystical image only becomes true and real in Christianity.

But it is a question whether the original Hebrew text read differently after all. How otherwise would the Septuagint, the Greek rendering of the Old Testament, put: "In the sun He (God) has pitched his tent."? It says that God has chosen the sun as His tent to dwell in, and not that He has given to the sun a dwelling at the ends of the world, i.e. in the ocean. The Greek word for tent (*skene*) is of the same root as that used in the prologue of St. John's gospel: "The Word became flesh and dwelt (lit. "pitched His tent") among us". St. John implies that the place where God dwells—which in the desert had been the tabernacle ("tent") of the Covenant—has been moved into Jesus of Nazareth. His human body is now the sacred "tabernacle of God among men". It appears that the Greek translators of the third and second century B.C. worked from a Hebrew text in which the sun was declared the tabernacle of God, in accordance with ancient "cosmic" religion. It is quite possible that the later Jewish orthodoxy altered this text, because it struck the orthodox rabbis as too "pagan". This surmise is confirmed, if one observes that the Greek translation of Solomon's Prayer for the dedication of the Temple contains a line (I Kings; 8, 12 – 8; 53 in the Septuagint) which is completely missing in the usual Hebrew bibles of today. Are we to believe that the translator simply invented that line? The usual Hebrew text says: "The Lord said that he would dwell in the thick darkness. I have surely built thee an house to dwell in . . ." The

Greek Septuagint reads: "The Lord has given the Sun in the sky for our knowledge. He said that He Himself would dwell in the darkness . . ."

It seems that these remarkable words testifying to an age-old sun-worship have simply been excised. It was for Solomon to realize that the time was at hand when the Spirit of the Sun would transfer His dwelling place into the interior darkness of the human soul. Solomon's temple was a prophecy of the body of Jesus, in which the Glory of God should dwell. In his prayer of dedication Solomon proclaimed the crucial transition from an epoch which observed the divine Presence radiating into man from without, from the cosmos, to a new epoch which would receive God as a Presence, indwelling in man.

The 19th Psalm which is described as "a Psalm of David" belongs still to the time *before* Solomon. Thus the second section of the Psalm, which is inspired by the recognition of the mysterious relationship between the "Son"-God and the Sun, could be rendered as follows:

> *His tent, He pitched it in the disc of the Sun.*
> *And He—as a Bridegroom goes forth from his*
> *   bridal chamber,*
> *Rejoicing as a strong hero to run his race.*
> *His going forth is from the end of heaven,*
> *And to the ends again He closes the circle.*
> *Nothing is hid from his fiery glow.*

III

THE HOLY BOOK

After these verses, full of the powers of nature, the Psalm takes on a quite different tone. It turns away from star and sun and becomes a hymn on the Law. It thus loses in colour, in elemental force that overwhelms the heart; it becomes paler, more abstract.

Critical investigation is therefore of the opinion that this praise of the Law was added to the powerful Psalm of nature in a later, decadent period. However the matter may stand, this Hymn on the Law belongs in any case to the 19th Psalm and we may find that it is nevertheless a true completion of the preceding part.

In the starry heavens—God the Father; in the sun—God the Son. With the Holy Book we enter, as it were, into the yet future sphere of the Holy Spirit. And since the working of the Holy Spirit is something that is still to come, we cannot be surprised if the third part of the Psalm is more abstract, less vigorous and natural. Yet this part, too, possesses its distinct beauty.

At the beginning of the Psalm the heavens and stars are extolled as the great manifestation; there the heavens are the book. In the third part of the Psalm this is reversed and in the book the heavens are discovered. "And when your hands unroll some parchment rare, all Heaven descends and opens out before you"—even if that dry and dusty bookworm, Wagner, speaks these words in Goethe's Faust, they are nevertheless a kind of reflection of genuine joy of the mind, genuine delight in knowledge given through the opening book of wisdom. This dried-up scholarship of Faust's amanuensis is noticeable in the old Jewish Rabbi's study of the Law. But the words of the Psalm, which speak of the blessedness which springs from the meditative study of the inspired holy texts have nevertheless something valid for all time, quite apart from the "Scribe" element. Thus in Christianity they can become alive and true for us. So, for instance, St. John's Gospel can become a book for us today in which "all heaven descends to us".

This eulogy of the holy Scriptures is cast in a form which divides into exactly twelve sentences (six double sentences). Something of the ordering of the starry heavens lies in this twelve-hood. The soul surrendered in devotion to the Law feels the harmonies of the star-world stream into it, bringing peace.

The world-ordering of the Lord is without
flaw, making peaceful the soul.

> *The testimony of the Lord creates spirit-*
> *confidence, making wise the simple.*
> *The statutes of the Lord are righteous,*
> *rejoicing the heart.*
> *The ordained goal of the Lord is clear,*
> *enlightening the eyes.*
> *The fear of the Lord cleanses through and*
> *through, enduring for ever.*
> *The precepts of the Lord are grounded in truth,*
> *uniting in righteousness with one another.*

These twelve statements are followed by a comparison which once more gathers the whole mood together and in its forcible imagery would make us feel that the joy of the spirit does not yield to the joy of the senses, but can surpass them in intensity of happiness.

> *Nobler than the noblest gold; sweeter than*
> *the sweetest honey.*

Gold was seen at all times as the transitory symbol of the sunlike light of wisdom. Honey in ancient times was something like the food of the mysteries. The Risen One, according to St. Luke's account, partook of honey as well as fish. According to the Psalm the Holy Book mediates the gold of wisdom and the most exquisite blessedness.

IV

THE HUMAN BEING

Having touched upon the three spheres of manifestation of the Father, the Son and the Spirit, now at the end the Psalm leads to the *human being* who turns back to *himself* out of the depths of his absorbed contemplation of the divine mysteries. And just as the first verses spoke of the resounding of the stars, of the Word of God sounding out from the Heavens, which is heard by the

inwardness of man, so the Psalm ends with the desire that likewise the inner word of man may be heard above in the heavens.
This is not presumption, but a presentiment of the dignity to
which man is called, in which he can only be fully established
through Christ, i.e. that he may not only "hear" but may also
"speak" as spirit to spirit, to God. Even as in the Lord's Prayer,
the petitioner passes over from selfless absorption in the great wish
which is wished on behalf of the Divine (Thy Name . . . Thy
Kingdom . . . Thy Will . . .), and only then comes to his own needs
and necessities, so at the end of Psalm 19 man enters into the
sphere of his own destiny. From being absorbed in prayer he
emerges again and comes to himself. But he has himself become a
different being. He has come to know the bliss of the higher life.
At the same time, however, he has acquired deeper insight into his
own inner nature and the perils and threats confronting it. He
knows that much of our wrong-doing never enters our consciousness. He knows of much that "wanders by night through the laby-
rinth of the breast unknown, unheeded by man". He has gained
impressions of the working of the opposing powers; for the old
law holds good that the devil, too, always draws nearer to us if we
have been able to take a step towards God. And let it once more be
repeated: the words of the Psalm reveal their full and right significance only in Christianity.

> *Moreover by them (the precepts of the Lord) is thy servant*
>   *enlightened,*
> *And he who keeps them in his soul reaps God's reward.*
> *Hasty actions—who is conscious of them?*
> *Cleanse Thou me from unknown faults,*
> *Preserve thy servant from the Powers of arrogance,*
> *Let them not gain dominion over me;*
> *Then I have part in the eternal*
> *And am purified from great transgressions.*
> *May my words find echo in the heavens,*
> *May the meditation of my heart reach unto thee,*
> *O Lord, rock-foundation of my Self, and my redeemer!*

The Seven Thunders

I

A heavy storm is approaching over the sea. The devout man of
the Old Testament lets his gaze rest upon the threatening masses
of cloud in solemn and anxious expectation, as befits the reception of some great revelation.

Then comes a flash of lightning, flaming over the whole sky.
It rends the clouds. It rends, too, a curtain before the searching
eye. The soul knows that it is rapt away from the earthly world.
Vanished are earth, sea, thunderclouds. In mighty visions the ritual
in heaven appears, Divine Worship as it is solemnized by those
who dwell in the higher worlds.

> *Bear to the Lord, ye Sons of God,*
> *Bear to the Lord revelation and power!*
> *Bear to the Lord the reflection of His Name!*
> *Offer Him worship in holy vesture of light!*

II

The vision of the heavenly High Mass fades. Among deepening
rolls of thunder the curtain closes again. The soul returns from
its ecstasy to the earthly body, sees again earth, sea, stormclouds
and hears the thunder which now follows the forewarning lightning. But now, sanctified by the vision, the soul is able to give the
thunder its right name—"the voice of the Lord" (*qôl Jahve*). For

48

the Hebrews this was a name for thunder. Seven times the rolling *qôl Jahve* occurs in the Psalm. It may perhaps be rendered "thunder-tone".

> *Thunder-tone of the Lord over the sea.*
> *The God of glory thunders;*
> *The Lord over the great waters;*
> *Thunder-tone of the Lord, full of strength,*
> *Thunder-tone of the Lord, full of majesty.*

The storm moves slowly over the leaden sea. The voice of Jahve over the waters—memory arises of the beginnings of Creation, how once the Spirit of God brooded over the waters like a cloud. It was pregnant with creative lightning—thoughts and powerful thunder-words; below it the expectant elements yielding in obedience.

III

The thunderstorm moves towards the land. It takes its way over the hills of the coast to the desert of Kadesh.

> *Thunder-tone of the Lord—he cleaveth the cedars.*
> *He cleaveth, the Lord, the Cedars of Lebanon;*
> *He maketh them leap like calves,*
> *The mountains of Lebanon and Sirion,*
> *Like young unicorns,*
> *Thunder-tone of the Lord sendeth forth cleansing*
>   *fires,*
> *Thunder-tone of the Lord shaketh the wilderness.*
> *He shaketh, the Lord, the desert of Kadesh.*
> *Thunder-tone of the Lord maketh the hinds to calve,*
> *Sheddeth leaves from the forests.*

From the sea to the land—the solid land is the realm of man's existence. All that in primeval beginnings was still pliable and heaving ocean is hardened and solidified in the earthly element.

The world trembles before the creative word of the Highest. What has taken shape on earth feels itself called in question when the Eternal speaks new words of power. The Sons of God in the heights solemnize the High Mass, earthly man feels himself brought to judgment.

That which is mortal groans in its foundations. The Psalm shows this in its manifold pictures. Age-old cedars, towering trees are struck by lightning and split asunder. Who can behold this and not be gripped by the gravity of the Last Judgment? The mountains tremble, rocked by an earthquake. In rich metaphor the Psalm compares them to skipping calves. Branches and leaves are torn from the trees by the tempest. The elemental pressure of what is taking place seizes the beasts of the forest, penetrating them through and through.

In seven mighty thunder-claps, three over the sea, four over the land, the storm passes over. One is reminded of the seven thunders of the Apocalypse of St. John, "Then seven thunders uttered their voices" (Apoc. 10; 3).

IV

On earth there is excitement, shock, shattering. That which is mortal groans in its foundations. The seven thunders have sounded. The soul which had trembled in its mortal part turns from the picture of the groaning uprooted forests, and lifts itself to the eternal. "But that which is immortal begins to shine more brightly, and know itself."

> And in his temple—all that is his, cries:
> Gloria!
> The Lord—above the flood he sits enthroned.
> Yea, throned is he, the Lord, a King in eternity.
> The Lord—he will give strength to his people.
> The Lord—he will bless his people with peace.

The Psalm ends where it began: in the heavenly sanctuary.

There, above, resounds the *"Gloria in excelsis"* of the heavenly hosts. The Eternal is throned in tranquillity above the flood—with the mention of which the earthly, catastrophic storm once more appears, dying away in violent downpour of rain as in the days of the flood itself.

It is impressive in the Apocalypse of St. John to observe how in the midst of the visions of disaster chasing each other, the picture of the heavenly throne appears over and over again, giving us the assurance of an eventual guiding of events. So here, too, the tranquil enthronement of the Eternal over the storms is presented in magnificent contrast.

The last word of this Psalm of storm is "peace". The storm is followed by the rainbow, the divine token of the covenant. This peace is not weak or cowardly. The human being who has passed through the storms and has become conscious of his immortal being feels his passage through the tempest as an increase of inner strength. So, too, his journey through the apocalyptic catastrophes effects an increase of powerful spirit-will. "The Lord will give strength to his people." The word of peace follows upon this word of strength. *"Gloria in excelsis"* is answered by *"et in terra pax"*—the peace on earth. Throughout the storms man knows himself to be united with the One throned in eternal majesty. The divine tranquillity throned above becomes a peace full of strength in the human heart below.

APPENDIX

"THE HEAVENLY RITUAL"

Those who take part in the heavenly worship are called in the original text *bene elim*, i.e. "Sons of God", not only "ye mighty". The gods of the ancient religions are beings from the ranks of the heavenly hierarchies, the angelic ranks of a ninefold order.

They are also spoken of in Psalm 89: "And the heavens shall

praise thy wonders, O Lord, and thy faithfulness in the congregation of the saints. For who in the clouds can be compared unto the Lord? An exalted God is he in the assembly of the saints, great and feared of all that are about him. O Lord God of Hosts, who is like unto thee?" (89; 5–8). Thus the vision of ancient times saw the God who speaks the great "I Am" in the midst of numberless hierarchical beings, for it is these that are meant by the "saints" in Psalm 89. It does not refer here to righteous men who have reached perfection, but to high beings from the ranks of the angels. Those standing in His presence partake in His holiness, as for instance the Seraphim whom Isaiah hears intone the great "Holy, Holy, Holy" in his Vision. (Isaiah 6.)

The Sons of God bear to Him the light of revelation (Glory, *Kabod*) and power. God has graciously poured forth His being into the world and they reflect it back to Him in gratitude. Divine thoughts and divine will-forces are reflected, as it were, in the world, and the beings of the angelic ranks mediate this divine reflection.

In Psalm 96, which extols apocalyptically the Coming of the Divine, almost the same words are to be found.

There is, however, the difference that men and indeed the whole of mankind are considered worthy to enter into this heavenly act of worship. Psalm 29 does not yet take this human possibility into consideration. It sees only the worship of the Angels.

In the last two Psalms the "Light-vesture" is mentioned. The one who turns to the Highest in prayer and sacrifice is clothed in Light. Ancient wisdom spoke of the fact that the one who worships receives a reflected splendour of the One who is worshipped. The Light-garment of holiness is the heavenly prototype of the priestly robes.

A Summer Song of Praise

PSALM 65

I

An inner mood of peace, relaxed and calm, breathing forth joy—
and outside, the ripeness of nature in all its fullness: these two are
woven harmoniously together in the 65th Psalm.

"Praise waiteth for thee, O God"—literally "Quietness is a
song of praise to thee". The soul turns towards the Divine in the
silence of devotion. "Unto thee shall the vow be performed".
The full range of this second sentence is perhaps not immediately
apparent to the modern reader. What sort of religious feeling lies
behind it? We regard it as an offence when someone promises
something and fails to fulfil the promise. We are willing to allow
that small children cannot be expected to make binding promises.
But it is different with adults, for a truly grown-up person is not
at the mercy of changing moods and feelings. The more the individual Ego develops in a human being, the more reliable and
constant he will be in all the changes of life. If man were only a
being of passing temporal nature, he would neither be capable
of faithfully remembering the past nor of carrying out with
firm will aims for the future. Anyone who is able to fulfil a
promise given perhaps a long time before, has built out of the
powers of eternity a bridge across the changing waves of time.
A religious vow was a means of education in the perception of
these powers of eternity. Whoever fulfilled a promise had at
that moment a meeting with himself as a being of eternity, above
and beyond all that is temporary and passing. He felt confirmed
and strengthened in the timeless core of his own being. And he

53

felt accepted by God through this fulfilment. Thus the Psalmist felt that his vow returned to the realm of eternity, and drew with it into that realm him who had fulfilled it. "Unto thee shall the vow be fulfilled". The Hebrew word for "fulfil" is the same root-word which also means "peace" (*shalom*).

A further experience grew out of the fact that man's activity in the sphere of eternity finds its way to God. That is God "hears prayer". Our endeavours towards the eternal sphere are not lost. They are taken up, accepted. Whether our prayers are "answered" is a secondary matter. "Thou hearest prayer." Just at this point the Psalm does not stop at our own ego. It recognizes the fact that every experience of the divine openness to our prayers lifts the one who prays above his own personality into the universal human sphere. "Unto thee shall all flesh come." The ear of God is open to all souls incarnated in an earthly body and suffering from the limitations of material existence.

The thought of the "flesh", the temporary sheath of the being of man, suggests the further thought of human failure and guilt: "As for our transgressions thou shalt purge them away". A power comes from the divine world which can overcome them. Something is dimly perceived here which was only realized at last in Christ.

This premonition of a future redemption from sin gives rise to the saying which follows: "Blessed is the man whom Thou choosest". This "choosing" should not be thought of in the sense of an abstract theory of "predestination", any more than the saying in the Gospels which seems to give precedence to those who are "chosen" over those who are "called". All higher experience has two aspects. "I shall know even as I am known". "I will sup with him, and he with me." The one side of the truth, "I want God" is far outshone by the other side, "God wants me", in the living experience of a devout soul. So also the fact that the devout soul has made a decision for God is completely overshadowed by the overpowering impression that God, on His side, has chosen the soul.

A further experience is linked with the sense of being "chosen".

It is the feeling that God is near. God is everywhere, certainly.
But His nearness is capable of a strengthening, an intensification.
This feeling of nearness can be enhanced until it becomes more
and more a sense of being at home in divine realms. Or, as the
Psalm expresses it, whoever is near to God may "dwell in Thy
courts: we shall be satisfied with the goodness of Thy house,
even of Thy holy temple." Here again the Psalm does not remain
caught in self-centred mysticism, but presses on to a higher social
consciousness, in the sphere of community. Just where the first
section of the Psalm rises to its height, to unity of being, Communion, the "we" appears over and above the individual. This
first part might perhaps be rendered:

> Silence toward Thee is a song of praise,
>   Thou God of Sion.
> The vow fulfilled—it unites in peace with Thee.
> Thou hearest prayer.
> To Thee shall all flesh come.
> Our failures grow over us,
> Our sins—Thou coverest them.
> Blessed is he whom Thou choosest,
> To whom Thou dost grant Thy presence.
>   He will dwell in Thy courts.
> We may be satisfied with the goodness of Thy house,
> With the holiness of Thy Temple.

II

The second part leaves the inner world of mystical and sacramental life and turns to the destiny of mankind, to world history.
In the otherwise peaceful Psalm an apocalyptic thunder becomes
audible. "Terrible" is the divine judgment which "answers" from
above the deeds and misdeeds of men. Eternal righteousness cannot do otherwise, it must re-act. The Godhead appears in history
as the guiding power in the life of nations over the whole earth.
The signs of the times are its beckoning gestures.

But just as in Beethoven's Pastoral Symphony the storm casts only a passing shadow over the bright summer day, so in this second part the mood of gratitude and joy breaks through again.

With terrible earnestness dost thou answer us in
   righteousness, O God, our Help.
Who by his strength setteth up the mountains,
   being girded with might.
Who stilleth the noise of the seas,
   the noise of the waves,
   the tumult of the peoples.
They who dwell in the uttermost parts turn away in awe
   at Thy tokens.
Thou makest the outgoing of the morning and evening
   to rejoice.

III

The third part turns to Nature, giving us one of the most beautiful pictures of Nature in the Bible. It describes how God visits the earth in the fructifying rain. It was not foolish superstition when the people of ancient times saw in rain the fructification of the earthly world by the heavenly. There was a time when the Divine still revealed itself to men directly in Nature. Expressions like "trees of God" or "river of God" were still meant quite literally. The inner and outer world were not yet separated from each other in human consciousness. So men still saw in the full-flowing river the very life-stream of God.

Through this ancient power of vision the "year" was also regarded as a living spiritual being, which revealed itself in time, and at the climax of its life was crowned by God. It stands before us in spiritual, ensouled corporality, and is not the merely abstract concept of a calendar.

That which is experienced in the first section as inward and sacramental, the divine Goodness which offers itself in Communion, comes again in the third section as mythical, tremendous, in

the life of Nature seen as though from outside. The Authorized
Version says: "Thy paths drop fatness". But the literal sense is
"chariot tracks", the underlying visionary picture being the
chariot of God which travels through the land bestowing fruitfulness wherever it goes.

"Thou blessest the springing up thereof". Whoever can really
bless is able to set free from his own soul a power which remains
henceforth with the one he has blessed. A blessing is not a "mere
word", but the real passing on of inward power. God has spoken
as it were a part of His divine soul into the being of the plant, so
that it can grow.

The hills and meadows are also seen in this religious way as
living beings. "The pastures are clothed with flocks." The animals add yet another covering to the green vesture of the plants.
A flock of grazing sheep is like a garment drawn over the earth.
And just as the green grass lays a covering of "life" as a fine
etheric garment over the otherwise bare earth, so in the soul-life
of the grazing flocks another, a soul-sheath, is woven above it.
Lastly, the grateful and happy minds of men come also into the
landscape, and add to the etheric life and the soul-activities of the
animals the human soul-life which is open to the divine spiritual
world. "The little hills rejoice on every side."

This religious joy in Nature unites beautifully with the inward
silence of the Temple at the beginning of the Psalm. The three
kingdoms of divine revelation have now been traversed: the
sphere of the Holy Spirit in the mystic-sacramental inner life, the
realm of the Son in the drama of world history, the kingdom of
the Father in the natural world; thus in each of the three sections the word "God" is spoken once. In this Psalm it is not the
stern name of Jahveh, but "Elohim", the name which bears within it the whole rich fullness of the divine powers.

Thou visitest the earth,
Waterest it, enrichest it greatly.
The river of God is full of water.
Thou preparest the corn,

Yea, Thou givest it strength.
Thou waterest the ridges,
Thou settlest the furrows,
Thou makest soft with showers.
Thou blessest the springing up thereof.
Thou crownest the year with Thy goodness.
The tracks of Thy chariot drip with abundance.
They drip on the pasture of the wilderness.
The hills are girdled with joy.
The meadows are clothed with flocks.
The valleys are covered with corn.
There is shouting and singing.

An Autumnal Song of Pilgrimage and Homecoming

PSALM 84

I

When summer comes to an end, cold and darkness slowly come to mind again, unnoticed at first, but with gradually increasing penetration. Human beings feel more strongly the need of a home as shelter for the winter. "Woe to him who has no home", says Nietzsche in his autumnal poem entitled "Vereinsamt". ("Lonely.") The more modern man feels uprooted and homeless in his outer life, the more he should feel called upon to seek his true home in a higher world. If he succeeds in taking root there inwardly, this "homecoming" helps him to take up the destiny of his unsafe and uncertain earthly pilgrimage with new courage.

These two things, the finding of a home in the eternal and courage for the earthly path, are wonderfully expressed in the 84th Psalm. Its designation "A Song over the Wine-Press, by the Sons of Korah" marks it as a song for autumn, for, as has already been explained in connection with Psalm 8, the Hebrew text does not indicate on the "Gittith" (guitar, zither?) as in the Authorized Version, but "over the winepress". Thus an autumnal mood is indicated though in a different way from that in Psalm 8.

> *How love-begetting are Thy dwelling places*
> *O Lord of the resplendent hosts.*
> *My soul is full of longing,*

59

Yea, it faints with longing for the courts of the
    Lord.
My heart, my whole body
    are thrilled by God who is Life itself.
The bird has found his home
    the swallow her nest where she may lay her young.
Thy altars! O Lord of the Radiant Hosts,
Thou King and Thou God of my Being.
Blessed they who dwell in Thy house
    They sing ever Thy praise.

                               Selah.

These verses may still be a valid expression of ritual worship
for us. We too know that wherever our altars stand is "home"
for us. Certainly God is everywhere. But it is a fact of the most
ancient and fundamental experience that the earthly environment of Man may become especially open and transparent for
the presence of the supersensory world in places that have been
set apart for worship. Earthly space is enclosed in a higher spiritual space. The Psalmist is conscious that the whole of Man is
affected by this sensory-supersensory event; not only the soul,
but also the heart, the actual Ego-centre, and even the "flesh".
The earthly body also shares in the stream of life which can be
felt issuing from God. It has already been noticed by several commentators how beautifully a trustful feeling of being at home
with the divine is woven together with a reverent humility in this
Psalm. The idyllical, peaceful picture of the swallow which has
found a place for her nest, is followed by a glimpse of the greatness and majesty of the divine: "my King and my God". The
"Lord Sabaoth" means literally the Lord of the "shining hosts",
by which we may think of the visible world of stars as well as of
the heavenly hosts of the angelic realms which belong to them.

    The first section of the Psalm ends with the word "Selah". It
is not quite clear what this means. The Greek translation says
Dia-psalma, which would indicate a musical interlude echoing
the mood of what had gone before.

II

The first part closes with a blessing promised to those who live constantly near to God. The blessing is taken up again at the beginning of the second section. (The Greek version uses the word *"makarios"*, which we know from the Beatitudes in the Sermon on the Mount.) But now it applies to anyone who goes courageously forward on pilgrimage. Here a strong "Michaelic" note comes into the Psalm.

> Blessed the man who finds his strength in Thee.
> Their hearts set on pilgrimage they pass through
>   the valley of tears.
> They turn it into a valley of springs.
> Full of blessings is he who points the way.
> They go from strength to strength, until they see
>   God in Sion.
> Lord, O God of the Radiant Hosts,
> Listen to my prayer, give ear to me,
>   Thou God of Jacob.
>
> Selah.

Whoever has found the "ways upwards" in his heart (Greek, *anabaseis*, Latin *ascensiones*) does not shrink from the necessary path of destiny through the Vale of Tears. This description of earthly life has not always had a healthy effect in religious circles. It may lead to a certain escapism. But the Psalm itself expresses no such cowardly mood. On the contrary, it says: Whoever has in his heart the possibility of upward progress will transform the earthly vale of tears into a place of blessing. He can draw on eternal springs even in the dreary desert, just as Christ said to the Samaritan woman that the water which He would give would spring up within man as a source of everlasting life. Through this the painful and dangerous pilgrimage of earthly life becomes a "going from strength to strength" for the pilgrim.

The text is now not quite clear. It may mean "one is seen by

God in Zion" or "one sees God in Zion". But however it is to be understood, it comes in the end to the same, i.e. the ancient mystical truth: "To know even as I am known". The vision of God is at the same time a being seen by God. Thus the end of the pilgrimage is a "seeing face to face".

III

From this prospect the Psalm leads back again to the feeling of "home" in the consecrated place. Again the prayer "Behold O God!" does not imply that the Omnipresent does not see everything. But the act of seeing is not felt here only from the aspect of perception. The seeing eye is not only a passive receiver of impressions, but it also sends out fine rays of light. The eye does not only see, it radiates. The late Professor Hermann Beckh,* has pointed out that just this radiance of light is expressed in the sound of the Hebrew word for "seeing" (raah). Thus the prayer "Behold" asks for the revelation of the divine radiance of light. To this is added the further request: "Illumine the countenance of Thine Anointed!"

The singer of this Psalm at that time may have been thinking of the King at Jerusalem, or of the High Priest. But these were both, after all, only the forerunners and representatives of Him who in the fullest sense is called "the Anointed". In the face of the Messiah, the Christ, the face of God became visible to us. "He who sees me, sees the Father". The creative light of God reaches its highest revelation in the countenance of the Saviour.

Once again the Psalmist is overcome by the consciousness of the infinite value of the experience of God in ritual worship: one day in the forecourt of the Temple outweighs a thousand other days. Once again the "Michael" note of the autumn festival is sounded in the theme of sun and shield. The words "glory and honour" which follow are connected with concrete and distinct

* At one time Professor of Oriental Languages at the University of Berlin, later priest of the Christian Community and one of its best Hebrew scholars.

experiences. Man is not yet complete. "It has not yet appeared what we shall be." (I John 3; 2.) There is still a cloud of unexhausted higher possibilities above our heads. That which is finally to become our personal being, our inmost possession, still hovers over us. When something of this creative cloud sinks down into a person, there is "grace". "Honour" (Heb. *kābôd;* Greek *doxa;* Latin *gloria*) is a radiance which is perceptible to a higher organ of sight. In the Old Testament it sometimes actually appears as a part of Man's being: "Wake up, my glory". (Psalm 57; 8). It is something like a fine supersensory light-organism, which awakens in Man when he shares in the grace that streams into him from above.

The Psalm ends with a third and last promise of blessing:

> *Behold us O God, Thou our shield,*
> *And send us Thy ray of light.*
> *Illumine the countenance of Thine Anointed.*
> *One day in Thy forecourts is more precious*
> *than a thousand others.*
> *Rather would I stay on the threshold of the house*
> *of my God, than live in the tents far away from Him.*
> *Yea, sun and shield is the Lord, our God.*
> *Grace and glory does he bestow.*
> *To those who live the good life*
> *He will never refuse His bounty.*
> *Lord of the Radiant Hosts,*
> *Blessed the man who puts his trust in Thee!*

The World of Sin and the World of Grace

Psalm 36

In verses 5–10 this Psalm contains a hymn which in its mythical greatness and mystical fervour may be counted among the high-lights of the Old Testament. In a rare example of "counterpoint" this Hymn to God is framed in a recital of how the evil in man becomes active from stage to stage.

I

The first verses give a concrete description of the psychology of the Fall of Man.

> *Evil whispers to the transgressor in his inmost heart.*
> *There is no fear of the divine in his eyes.*

The word "whisper" is generally used in the Prophetic Books for the inspiration of the voice of God. Here is a sinister antithesis to such divine inspiration. The powers of the adversary are also aware of how to instill something into man. Thus the serpent speaks to Eve. Thus the Devil puts it "in the heart" of Judas to be-tray the Lord (John 13; 2). The Psalm knows that in the evil im-pulses of man an objective spirit-world, outside man, plays its part.

After the heart comes the eye. The whisper of evil has insinu-ated itself into the heart; now the eyes become "bold". They lose reverence for the divine. They no longer behold the glory of the divine in the material world. Their vision is entangled in the vain show of appearances, and with all its cleverness becomes blind to the heavenly golden ground behind the objects.

The next verse is difficult to translate. Perhaps it reads: "Sin flattereth his eyes, that he findeth guilt and hatred." Flattery is so effective because it appeals to vanity. And then the man "finds" guilt and hate, falling into their realm without knowing how he does so.

Verse 3, passing outwards from the inner circle of the mind, now speaks of "words". "The words of his mouth are iniquity, wantonness and deceit. He hath left off to be wise and do good". The sacred character of "The Word" is lost, it falls a prey to the powers of lying. Wisdom and goodness are lost from the word. Cold cunning enters in their place, which with all its cleverness is ultimately "foolishness" before God (for in spite of all brilliant intellectuality the popular expression holds good, "stupid as sin"). And lovelessness, even hate, follow.

It is a significant expression that the man who has gone astray "ceases to be wise and good". Evil is nothing primary and original, it is not an attribute of man from the outset, it is, on the contrary, an "infection", as in fact we express with the words "sickness of sin". Man has been infected with a spirituality fundamentally foreign to him. Evil is "inhuman". It has come upon man like an illness. He is in danger of completely losing his primitive state, his innate divine nature. Therefore "he has left off", he has departed from, being truly wise and good. "He deviseth mischief upon his bed." Man companioned by his sleepless hours is a theme frequently found in the Psalms. It is not only in our "nervous" age, when it has become an illness, but even earlier we find man passing sleepless nights, driven round and round by consuming care, or filled by violent emotions which keep him awake. Dealing with sleeplessness is an important chapter of self-training. Such exercise is found in the Psalms: "The upright man meditates on the law day and night" (1; 2). "In the night my song is to him" (42; 8). "To show forth thy loving kindness in the morning and thy truth at night" (92; 2). Also from the Book of Job: "They cry that there is much oppression, and cry out by reason of the arm of the mighty, but none asketh: Where is God my maker, who giveth songs of praise in the night?" (Job 35; 9, 10).

3

From the poisoning of these silent hours in which man "upon his bed" is alone with himself, there logically proceeds the wicked deed in the light of day, "he setteth himself in a way that is not good". Therewith the evil that began with the inspiration in the heart and then invaded the sphere of words, henceforth penetrates into action. It is the treading of a "path". A path is entered upon with the first wrong deed, and one step follows another. All is in process of evolving, of movement. Through his power to be free man can give this or that direction to his own development. The first Psalm describes very clearly the "two paths".

"He rejecteth not evil"—Man loses the natural sense of strangeness that he first feels towards evil. A healthy body rejects by a right instinct food that is not good for it. So are we also fundamentally equipped with a feeling for what does not suit us, is not in accord with us, for what is foreign to our nature and does not belong to us. But in the sphere of moral action bad habits can gradually paralyse the sound instinct of defence. "He rejecteth not evil"—he loses the power of repulsing what is not of his nature.

II

A wonderful hymn to God now begins, apparently unconnected with what has gone before. We have been looking at the oppressive spectacle of how evil takes hold of man, and with inexorable logic works itself out from the mind into the word and from word to deed. This is depicted with deeply penetrating observation and knowledge of man. One could become alarmed at these reflections. How then is this sinister process to be countered?

The Psalm gives a grand and noble answer. Without concerning itself with the more obvious logical sequence of its sentences, it breaks off abruptly and speaks of something quite different, as if it wished to say: turning one's gaze resolutely to the positive and divine is the only remedy. The verses which then follow are all the more impressive through this striking contrast:

Lord, in the heavens—thy grace.
Thy truth—unto the clouds.
Thy righteousness—like mountains of God.
Thy judgments—a great deep.
To man and beast art thou a saviour.
O Lord, how excellent is thy grace.
Divine beings and sons of men put their trust in
*   the shadow of thy wings.*
They satisfy themselves in the abundance of
*   thy house.*
Thou givest them to drink of the river of thy
*   bliss*
For with thee is the fountain of life.
In thy light we see the light.

At the beginning of this hymn the Psalmist uses the name of God which holds the mystery of the I Am. And it is as if the speaking of this hallowed name leads his soul upwards in a mighty ascension.

"Lord, in the heavens—thy grace." The ardour which immerses itself in the divine is all the more powerful against the background of evil. It is like the sudden rending of a curtain. From the name of God the vision of His heavens unfolds. It is only a plausible notion that physical science and aeroplanes have got rid of "heaven". It is the same as if one fine day it was "discovered" that the Sistine Madonna was only a painted surface, that there was in fact nothing further of a corporal nature upon it or behind it. That takes nothing away from its importance, for it is a picture. A picture which points however to a reality of a higher order. So too the sky we see, in its vaulted arch, in its blue, in the changes of its phenomena of light, is a picture which is given to us and which loses nothing of its value through the explanations of physics and astronomy. To surrender oneself in contemplation of the heavens unlocks in one's inner being the worlds of God's grace, which are assuredly not "spatial".

For the Psalmist the heavens are the sphere in which the

Godhead is utterly and entirely "at home", by itself, in its own element, in which it can live undisturbed in its innermost essence. This innermost essence is known as "Grace".

"Thy truth—unto the clouds". The clouds too belong to the "heavens". How much exaltation and rapture have men felt in the devout contemplation of the lofty spaces of the clouds. But still, in this second line in contrast to the first ("In the heavens—thy grace") we have descended one stage and come nearer to the earth. In comparison with the starry heavens and the pure blue the clouds are nevertheless a transition and border region in which the heavens descend nearer to the earth.

Now why should precisely the cloud be combined with the experience of truth? For us the cloud is so often precisely something that veils, that conceals the view. But it was still living experience to the men of old that the cloud not only veiled but also revealed. Hidden forces of vision can be released in the soul by giving oneself up to the picture of the mysterious invisible hands of God at work in the changing forms of the clouds. The truth of God as of the eternal disposing One, the forming and transforming One, reaches from the upper heavens down to the realm of the clouds. The clouds carry down the active manifestation of the living God to us beneath and make it visible. Down as far as the clouds there still extends His "immediacy".

Grace and truth—we know these two significant words from the prologue of the Gospel of St. John. They are said of Him who had become flesh, "full of grace and truth".

What for our Psalm still belongs to cosmic spaces appeared for John for the first time in earthly form. "Grace and truth came by Jesus Christ." What the Psalm still beholds in the "above", removed from earth, for John actually entered the stream of historical human evolution.

The next line, the third, is again a descent: from the clouds to the mountains. And then we set foot on the solid earth.

Regarded from above, the mountain summit is indeed "earth". But for man in the valley, the mountain is something that still belongs to heaven. On mountain heights the ancients felt themselves in greater nearness to God's heaven. One who saw from below the sacred mount towering upwards was reminded of the eternal. The devout experiences of past millennia, of forgotten "fathers who have worshipped upon the mountain", surround such an expression as "God's mountains".

"Thy righteousness—like the mountains of God." A comparative "like" appears for the first time. Till now we were still in a sphere of divine "immediacy". Righteousness is for the Psalm an effect of the divine that has more connection with earthly than heavenly grace and truth. The sternness of an eternal righteousness looks down from the mountains of God upon the drifting changes below.

Still one more, a final descent, is accomplished: "Thy Judgments —a great deep". Great deep, in the original text: *thehom rabba*. *Thehom* is the primal flood, savouring of the weird, darkly chaotic, losing itself in dreadful darkness (Greek *abyssos*). *Thehom* is the totality of all nocturnal powers of Chaos, which in the form of the dragon Leviathan had to be thrust down by Jahve in the primeval world conflict (cf. Isaiah 51; 9) so that an orderly creation might arise.

Thehom rabba, the great deep, occurs significantly in the narrative of the Flood. Where man transgresses against measure and order, God punishes him by allowing the ancient powers of chaos to raise their head again, for though they were once vanquished, they were not destroyed. Then man is delivered over to the powers whose chains he has wantonly unloosed through his transgression. "All the fountains of the great deep were broken up . . ." (Genesis 7; 11).

This Flood, this fall of the iniquitous Atlantian magicians and "arrogant giants" (Book of Wisdom, 14; 6) is the classical example of divine judgment, the prototype of the court of justice.

> Grace and truth—God in heaven.
> Righteousness and Justice—God upon earth.

In other words: God as He can live out His true being by

Himself in His own archetypal world, and God as, by virtue of eternal law, He must show Himself on the earth inhabited by fallen mankind. God in His light-filled freedom on the one hand, and on the other hand, in His dark necessity. Only through Christ is the heaven of grace and truth carried down into the dark world which stands under judgment.

Heavens—clouds—mountains—depths of the sea. Grace—truth—righteousness—judgment. Mighty and of mythical greatness is this gradual descent from the freedom of God down to the lowest depths of necessity.

Into the sinister echoes of the flood, *thehom rabba*, some consolation is brought, reminiscent of the Ark of Noah. "To man and beast art thou a saviour". To the animals too, God's aid is promised here. Man has drawn the animals down with him into the fatal consequences of his fall into Sin. Hence he must not only desire the redemption of his own soul, but must also take to heart the destiny of the creatures.

This thought of God's help forms the transition to the mystical centre of the 36th Psalm. For the experience of divine grace is proclaimed in anticipation of what will at last be disclosed to man in full measure through Christ.

"Lord, how precious is thy Grace. God and sons of man shelter in the shadow of thy wings." In the original text, according to Hebrew grammar, the word *Elohim* probably belongs to the next line, so that the text employed by us reads: *Elohim*, that is, divine beings of the higher hierarchies, and sons of men shelter in the shadow of thy wings.

An experience of grace that goes beyond being sheltered is the Holy Meal through which the communion, the imparting of divine life, is received: "They satisfy themselves with the abundance of thy house. Thou makest them drink of the river of thy bliss. For with thee is the fountain of life". The "house" of God is the abode of His presence. Fallen man like the Prodigal Son in the parable, wasted his heritage far from his father's house, and in so doing has destroyed his "substance", falling into dire need. Divine grace will call man again to the table of its fulness, when in the company of higher Beings (*Elohim*) he eats the "bread of the angels" (Psalm 78; 25).

The "river of bliss" is the same as the river of Paradise spoken of in Genesis. "Bliss" in the original text is "Eden". It becomes very clear here in the Psalm, that in the description of Paradise one should never ask concerning its geographical whereabouts. The source of the river of Eden which represents flowing life, is "with thee".

Life as such is not visible to earthly eyes. They see only what is filled with life, not life itself. Flowing water is its image, and all natural life, however sacred and mysterious in itself, is again but the reflection of a still higher, truly supernatural life.

It is the spirit of St. John's gospel which we meet in this Psalm. While it was first the words "grace and truth" that made us think of the prologue of the Gospel of St. John, we now see how "light" is added to "life".

"In thy light we see the light." Simple as these words may sound, there nevertheless lies hidden in them a whole epistemology. It would be impossible for man to have real knowledge if the world confronted him as being entirely foreign to himself. The light of the world outside might shine upon us ever so brightly and clearly, yet it would simply run off the surface of our nature without finding the way into our inner being. But man himself participates in the light. He can behold the light of the world because he can meet it with his own inner human light, light uniting with light. By our very participation in the light, we are able to see the light.

This light, which is active in the thinking of man, is not his own, subjective light. Even as a single individual he has a share in the divine light itself. Therefore the light of thinking in man can be objectively valid for the world. "In thy light we see the light."

Similarly the 18th Psalm says: "Thou lightest my lamp" (Psalm 18; 28). Man has his own light, his "lamp". But God must illumine it for him by feeding the lamp with His own divine Light. A passage in Job points to a still earlier time when the light entrusted to man made no pretension to be his own, but was felt as still be-longing directly to God. Job desires to be back in the time "when God preserved me, when His lamp shone above my head". (Job 29; 3).

We participate in a light of vision and of knowledge because the Godhead that bears us is itself living in this light element of vision and knowledge. So says Psalm 94; 9: "He that created the eye, shall He not see?"

III

This mystical centre piece of Psalm 36 is followed by a concluding prayer which ends with an apocalyptic view of the fate of the wicked:

> *Continue thy grace unto them that know thee,*
> *And thy righteousness unto them that are upright*
>   *in heart.*
> *Let me not be trodden down by the foot of the proud,*
> *Nor the hand of the Godless drag me to the ground.*

The personal enemies and opponents of the Psalmist become the symbol for the powers of evil that break in upon man and against whom he hides himself in the divine Grace.

> *There—they are already fallen, the workers of iniquity.*
> *They are cast down and shall not be able to rise.*

These lines have the character of a vision, of an apocalyptic view. "There—they are fallen!" It is the apocalyptic perfect tense: in the spirit-vision something is accepted in advance as having already happened. So the Christ says in the Farewell Discourses—that is to say, before Gethsemane and Golgotha—"The Prince of this world is already judged". And, "I have overcome the world". It is the same in the Book of Revelation, where in Chapter 11 the songs of victory already resound in heaven, before the Antichrist

reaches the zenith of his power on earth. Whence comes this anticipation? Spirit-vision carries one into a region in which the decision has in fact already been made. It is only that a little time is
still needed until what has been decided in principle gradually
"arrives" upon the earth beneath.

Thus the Psalmist also sees the adversary as though already
fallen. Evil is in principle already "despatched", it is judged and
sentenced to death. Let it celebrate triumphs however great—the
truth of the apocalyptic vision stands.

The Great Confession

PSALM 51

I

It has been said that the greatest of evils is guilt. Adversity that meets us from without, through destiny, is, with all its pain and suffering, easier to bear than the sight of one's own guilt and its effect. All that transpires in the soul of one who has done wrong and who yet yearns and strives for the divine blessing—this is the content of the well-known "penitential" Psalm 51. Tradition says that it is a prayer of David after his sin with Bathsheba:

> *Have mercy upon me, O God, according to thy loving*
> *kindness;*
> *According unto the multitude of thy tender mercies blot out my*
> *sins.*
> *Wash me thoroughly from my guilt,*
> *And cleanse me from my transgressions.*

The trinity of sin, guilt and transgression is to be found at the beginning of the 32nd Psalm, "Blessed is he whose transgression is forgiven, whose sin is covered. Blessed is the man unto whom the Lord imputeth not iniquity". The word that we render by "sin" is the gravest of these three. It denotes an offence committed deliberately, whereas "transgression" means rather sins of passion or weakness. "Blot out my sins." In the original text "blot out" is a word that one can very well use for obliterating what has been written. May the sin be effaced like the writing in a book. That is more than an ingenious image. With all that man does, feels and thinks, he makes something like "entries" in an infinitely fine

74

cosmic substance. Something is detached from us and continues in the universe beyond our reach and has its consequences.

We have no longer control over these effects of our deeds which have passed out into the cosmos. The prayer of the Psalm can really only be fulfilled through Christ. He alone, by virtue of his sacrifice has the power to blot out the objective consequence of our sins for the universe, if we unite ourselves with Him, as with the Lamb that takes upon Himself the "sin of the world".

"Wash me from my guilt." "Wash" in the original text is a word used for the washing of a garment. Man has darkened the shining of his finer nature by sin. He has spotted the vesture of his soul and lacks the "wedding garment".

"Cleanse me." This does not mean the washing of a garment but the direct cleansing of the body. It is here a question (using the image of the body) of "us ourselves". With the wrong that we commit we injure ourselves. But it does not remain our private affair, since it moves out of the private sphere of our inner personal realm into the finer sheaths surrounding us and "blackens" their innate brightness; the sin acquires an effect in the universe, for the whole of our body and soul nature is a fragment of the universe which is entrusted to us as our own. The cleansing of the body and the washing of the clothing has to do with the consequences of sins for ourselves and for the sheaths which belong to our being and which form a kind of intermediary between our inner nature and the world outside.

But furthermore there are effects which transcend ourselves and the fragment of the world entrusted to us and which belong to the universe outside. These are not only the changes which we have effected physically in the world through our action. What we have done in the visible world is, after all, in spite of its often dreadful reality, only a sort of image of the injury we have done to the hidden spiritual substances of the world and which now stands as a writing in the Cosmic Book and looks at us accusingly.

For I acknowledge my sins and my transgressions are ever before me.

Against thee, thee alone have I sinned
And what is evil in thy sight, that have I done,
That thou mightest be justified in thy verdict
And be clear when thou judgest.

The Psalmist has become fully conscious of the wrong he has
done. It stands before his eyes and afflicts him. "Against thee, thee
only have I sinned." Tibi soli peccavi—herein lie the true depths
of his confession. First and foremost the sin is committed against
God Himself; it is only in the second place that it is directed to this
or the other person who is concerned. We are guilty towards anyone whom we injure, but above all towards God. We also hear in
the Act of Consecration★ that our deviations, our denials of the
divine Being, our weaknesses, find their way into the depths of the
Ground of the World. Rudolf Steiner speaks of the pain that we
cause to higher beings through our mistakes and failings. Such an
indication can make this wonderful, intuitive Psalm alive and real
for us. "Against thee alone have I sinned."

Behold, I was shapen in iniquity
And in the realm of sin did my mother conceive me.
Behold, thou desirest truth in hidden things,
Thou makest me to know secret wisdom.

When the Psalm speaks in these words of "original sin" this is
not, as it were, pleading "extenuating circumstances", but it is a
recognition of hidden circumstances. The human being, thrown
out of the *naïveté* of his matter-of-course existence by the feeling of
guilt, has become sensitive to the fact that he and the whole of his
earthly human nature is from the start incompatible with the divine world. He sees himself gripped in a vast sequence of events,
fettered for thousands of years in a state of guilt and wrongdoing
from which he cannot become free without divine help. Man
knows himself to be guilty not only of individual offences which

★ "The Act of Consecration of Man" is the name of the Communion Service in the
Christian Community.

can be named and enumerated, but he knows and feels that his whole mode of life is not consistent with the divine world. To a superficial view sin consists only in single acts, and if these had been left undone man would have continued "in order". Only a deeper wisdom that penetrates below the surface can recognize that the whole condition of man from the beginning is infected by the sickness of sin.

Just as this "from the start" is something transcendent, something that belongs to humanity over and above the individual, so too, nothing but a divine impulse of a transcendent order can release man from these chains. This came about through Christ. The devout man of the Old Testament is praying in the hope of the approaching Redeemer, when at the beginning of the Psalm he calls upon divine grace. This grace which enters fully into the earthly world through Christ does not mean that God merely throws overboard the reckoning of justice and replaces it with arbitrary action. No, not that. But he brings a new dimension into the calculation. The iron law of cause and effect is not annulled, but the result becomes different through the inclusion of quite a new power. This new factor which gives the whole situation a new physiognomy is "grace", the Christ. This grace causes an additional force to flow into man, through which the consequences of evil can be carried and transformed to good.

Grace does not relieve us of our own efforts. But it must be obvious that without it human entanglement in evil which far transcends our own power to master it cannot be overcome.

The 51st Psalm will only become fully true and concrete in the framework of the New Testament. In Christ appears the Grace which can counteract the Fall and its consequences, which have long since become too much for man. With the sight of the suffering God on the Cross man first becomes fully conscious of what in a sort of dreaming presentiment is expressed in the Psalm, "Against thee, thee alone have I sinned."

II

Purge me with hyssop and I shall be clean,
Wash me that I may be whiter than snow.

Here begins the actual prayer for transformation. The imagery is to be understood in reference to the rites of purification in the Old Testament. Aspersion by means of a hyssop branch (which served as a sort of holy water sprinkler) was commanded in the case of leprosy and contact with a corpse. We must imagine the whole dreadfulness of the Eastern disease of leprosy, where a man's entire body becomes rotten bit by bit. The leper decaying in the living body, the corpse which falls into decay; in both cases there is destruction of the body, and this dread of destruction was felt to be connected with the sickness of sin. The hyssop branch played a part in banishing this horror through the ritual of consecrated aspersion. The one who has become conscious of his sinfulness feels himself delivered up to the powers of leprosy and decay. He "tastes" death in himself. So he prays for purification.

One should not quickly dismiss the ancient rites of washing and cleansing as mere formalities. Inner and outer experiences were not so separated in those times. Bodily cleansing did not remain without effect on one's inner nature. One could not undergo it without the process being continued to a greater or lesser degree inwardly. Even today we must not underestimate this effect. To be sure, outer cleanliness is not yet inner cleanliness, but it has nevertheless a conducive influence upon it.

"Whiter than snow". Snow gives a greater experience than anything else of unearthly, shining purity. White as snow is the raiment of the Easter angel (Matt. 28; 3). In the seventh chapter of Revelation, St. John describes his vision of the perfected saints. They are clothed in shining white raiment which they "have washed in the Blood of the Lamb". A paradoxical picture, which demonstrates that through accepting what proceeds from Golgotha the whole nature of man is purified and illumined. Only the "Blood of the Lamb" will bring about what the pre-Christian

Psalm is here imploring: "Wash me, that I become white as snow".

The Psalm passes over from the world of light to the world of sound:

> *Make me to hear joy and gladness.*

When the human being radiates again like fresh snow, the heavenly music of rejoicing becomes audible to the inner ear. In the parable of the Prodigal Son there is also the sound of singing and dancing at the great feast of reunion. It is the jubilation of the heavens when man is given back, cleansed and transformed, to the spheres of his origin. The theme of gladness goes through the whole of the 15th chapter of St. Luke's Gospel which proclaims in three parables how what is lost has been restored. "Rejoice with me." "Likewise there is joy in the presence of the angels of God." Consciousness of guilt takes away happiness. Anticipation of grace awakens joy. This goes through and through.

> *The bones which thou hast broken rejoice.*
> *Hide thy face from my sins,*
> *And blot out mine iniquities.*

The negative element of forgiveness is expressed here once more: the turning away of the divine countenance from our guilt, and thereby the cessation of the tormenting reproach that we feel when the divine gaze dwells on our faults. The following verses pass over entirely into the positive attitude. Not only are our sins blotted out, but a complete rebirth takes place through a new act of creation by God.

> *Create in me a clean heart, O God,*
> *And renew a spirit of firmness within me.*
> *Cast me not away from thy countenance,*
> *And take not the spirit of thy holiness from me.*
> *Restore unto me the joy of thy help*
> *And endow me with a spirit of free will.*

"Create in me a clean heart." Here the word *bara* stands for "create". It is a word seldom used, but occurs precisely seven times in the book of Genesis. Used here, it is to show that the transformation of fallen man is to be set beside the world's creation. The new creation is implanted in the innermost heart of man. And as the working of the Spirit belongs to the Creation, so too it belongs to the new creation of man. In Psalm 104 it says, "Thou sendest forth the breath of thy spirit and thou renewest the face of the earth". This renewing force of the divine spirit is to show itself here in man's inner being.

It is remarkable how in the 51st Psalm spirit is mentioned in a threefold manner. First it is the spirit of steadiness, firmness; with the creation of the pure heart, the spirit lifts us out of all vacillating to and fro, and makes us come to rest on the granite of eternity. The spirit of firmness—one might call this the Father-aspect of this trinity.

Then the Holy Spirit, connected with experience of the divine countenance; through the spirit of holiness man is enabled to stand face-to-face with God, is enabled to know the Divine as from spirit-being to spirit-being. Without the spirit of holiness he must faint away before this countenance, he could not hold himself upright in face of the personal consciousness of God turned towards him. "Take it not from me"—the gift of the Holy Spirit can also be lost. A guilty darkening of our being can banish us from His sight. We feel the infinite preciousness, the value of this Holy Spirit, and tremble at the prospect of being again deprived of it. It is just because full holiness will only be in man's complete possession at final consummation, that the beginning of our sanctification is something so delicate, so liable to attack and easily lost.

Finally the spirit of spontaneity, of "free-will of action" is connected with joy in divine aid. The word used in the original text as referring to the spirit, means also "noble", "distinguished", while its root means doing good spontaneously, out of one's own free will. Hence, "generous" and "distinguished", "noble". In distinction to the spirit of firmness and of holiness, it is here the spirit of the Son. The Son brings us the help of God ("help of God" is the meaning of the name "Jesus"). He helps man to live rightly as earthly personality and he unseals the power which does good not by compulsion of the law, but out of freedom, generously, from one's heart as an expression of one's own nature. In this lies indeed the true distinction and nobility of man as opposed to the compulsory work of a slave.

The spirit of firmness—the spirit of holiness—the spirit of spontaneity. It is one of the passages in the Old Testament where the mystery of the Trinity is clearly foreshadowed.

III

If man has become a new creature, he can have significance for others, for good. As one who has been born again and transformed, he can now also point the way to his fellow men.

> *Then I will teach thy ways to sinners,*
> *That those who go astray may turn to thee.*

Just because he has himself learnt to know guilt and for this reason has been able to gain all the deeper insight into the forces of healing and transforming possessed by the Godhead, he can now help others to find their way in life. That need not be a pretentious "teaching"; there is no need for words. The very character of his being has its own effect.

> *Deliver me from bloodguiltiness, O God, thou*
> *God of my true Self and my help,*
> *And my tongue shall sing aloud of thy righteousness.*
> *O Lord, open thou my lips that my mouth*
> *shall show forth thy praise.*

He who has injured his fellow men through misdeeds can, after his rebirth, be a help to them. Through rebirth he may even mean something positive for the divine world. As a sinner he was a being who served to conceal God and diminish His manifestation. Wherever something bad is present the divine is covered over and the adversary is revealed instead. The Psalm pleads that man may again become a being that manifests the divinity. In the long run there will be no other valid proof on earth that God exists except human beings reborn through the spirit. "Ye are the light of the world", says Christ to His disciples. People ought not to complain of the darkness and ungodliness of the world, for it is their own fault that it is dark; they are not shedding light. Man is the door through which God can enter the earthly world.

Generally speaking, we form a far too ordinary, vague and casual idea of what is meant by praising and extolling. This is a result of a regrettable inflation which has robbed the great words of religion of their value. To extol God—that means to bring Him to appearance, to manifestation, so to "densify" His divine presence that it again becomes discernible on earth. The 51st Psalm indicates that praising God is not a cheap matter. Otherwise the prayer would not have been uttered that God Himself should open our lips to His praise. It is not done by opening our mouth to speak edifying words. If the outpouring of our being, of which in fact words are only a part, is to extol God, then the higher world must itself make us worthy of it and give us its blessing.

We now understand why there is again a reference in this connection to "blood guilt". In the original text the word blood is given in the plural, "Deliver me from the guilty power and influence of blood-relationships." One must not narrow this down to merely one criminal act, as perhaps the murder by David of Uriah. All men are involved in a vast portentous association of guilty forces of the blood. Original sin is in the blood of the entire human race. "Take away from me the guilty blood-forces." This plural of blood which is grammatically impossible in English and other modern languages, is also found in the Greek of the New Testament, where St. John's Gospel speaks of "those which were born, not of blood (*haimata*), nor of the will of the flesh, nor of the will of man, but of God". (The blood of Christ redeems and replaces sinful powers of human blood.)

Only when the Blood of Christ becomes a power within us will we be able to join fully in the angels' song of praise which reveals God.

For thou desirest not sacrifice,
Else would I give it;
Thou delightest not in burnt offering either.
The true sacrifices of God are a devoted spirit
A devoted and humble heart, O God,
    thou wilt not despise.

The Temple ritual of the blood-offering is here turned inward. The Psalm stands at the threshold of an age when the sacrifice of an animal no longer called forth an inner experience by virtue of a primitive, magical feeling of being connected with it. The inward element begins to be detached. In early times one could not sacrifice one's external "possession"—perhaps a beast from the herd—without at the same time a part of the soul. The soul-force was objectified in this animal, streaming upward to the Godhead. This intimate connection was gradually lost. It has become fitting that man's capacity to think, feel and will should be offered to God.

The Psalmist who had this inward experience in advance of Old Testament times, had outgrown the epoch when animal sacrifices were fully justified. Their place is taken for him by the "broken" spirit and the broken "shattered" heart, as the text reads literally. The selfhood, formed by the Fall, always wants to shut itself off within its own narrow horizon. This exclusiveness must again and again be broken up so that we do not withdraw into our lower self and thereby shut out the true higher Ego which is destined for us.

    Show thy goodwill unto Zion:
    Build thou the walls of Jerusalem,
    Then shalt thou be pleased with the sacrifices of
      righteousness,
    With burnt offering and whole offering:
    Then shall they offer bullocks upon thine altars.

This conclusion has a strange sound after what has just been said about making the sacrifices an inward deed. It has been regarded as a later addition which was attached to the Psalm lest it

sounded heretical in view of the official Temple worship. It has
been thought that perhaps through these final orthodox sentences
the all too bold inwardness of an individualistic religious genius
was rendered harmless. This is not impossible. However these final
verses may have found their way there, they are nevertheless no
misrepresentation of the whole, in spite of a certain contradiction
of what has gone before. In fact, they are an important and significant addition, whether they are the work of the author or of a
strange hand. These final verses uphold the truth that the shattering experiences of sin and grace are not just a matter of "God and
the soul". After these inner processes it is salutary and compensa-
tory that at the close, attention is drawn to great, cosmic aims. The
city of Jerusalem becomes altogether a symbol in the Apocalypse
of St. John. The "heavenly Jerusalem" is the new, Christianized
earth. Even in the Old Testament Jerusalem begins to mean more
than a geographical name. In the Books of the Prophets, Zion,
Jerusalem, has become a symbolic concept, the epitome of a coming world of redemption and perfection. This is also in the background of the final words of the great Penitential Psalm. Every sin
is a contribution to the building of Babylon, the city of the Abyss
which is established apart from the divine world. The transforming of the sinner contributes to the building of the Holy City.

And the Temple Offering mentioned in the last verse? The
burnt offering and the whole offering? They establish the truth
that the inner sacrifice of a broken spirit and heart, which is pleas-
ing to God, is not alone sufficient. Even the most pious emotions
of the best of men could not release the human race from the overpowering entanglement of original sin. This could only be effected
through something that allows of no comparison—the sacrifice of
a God, the Deed of Golgotha. The Temple worship with its
blood-sacrifice was the forerunner of this unique Offering, which
then lives on upon the altars of Christendom. In the service at the
Christian altar the inner sacrifice, the devotion of spirit and heart
then comes into its own. But the inward sacrifice of man is only
the preparation for the fact that in the transubstantiation the sacrifice on Golgotha can live again. There is an organic union of the

seemingly contradictory elements of the 51st Psalm—the inward devotion of spirit and heart, the sacrificial offering of the inner faculties, and the great objective sacrifice of a God, surpassing all human possibility, the fulfilment of the ancient burnt offering and whole burnt offering.

In the Presence of Eternity

PSALM 90

I

The 90th Psalm, which bears the name of Moses, is one of the
most monumental in the whole book.

A prayer of Moses, the Man of God.

> *Lord, thou hast been our refuge in all generations.*
> *Before the mountains were brought forth or ever*
> *thou hadst formed the earth and the world,*
> *Even from everlasting to everlasting, O God,*
> *THOU ART.*

Just as in Genesis Moses is the seer who looks back, so here too
the Psalm opens by looking into the past. It scans the ranks of
generations. The family tree of descent in the Gospel of St. Luke
goes back to Adam, "which was the son of God". Here too the
Divine is reached in passing back through the ages.

High mountains are the representatives of eternity on the
earth. They soar upwards beyond what becomes and passes
away in time; throughout summer and winter they are crowned
with the eternal snows. Immutable, they look down upon the
ever changing human destinies in the valleys below.

Mountains, too, are subject to passing away, but it happens
so slowly and imperceptibly that we do not see it or realize it;
so that after all they are something "relatively eternal" upon
earth. The Psalm knows that even these primeval mountains
were once young, they were once "born", as the Hebrew has it.

In far past ages the earth was not so hardened and dead as it is to-day where life is only to be found in the separate living creatures. The earth itself was once the living mother of these organisms. All substance was then much finer, charged with life. Yes, the earth itself which brought forth the mountains, was also born, it once detached itself from the womb of the creative worlds of spirit.

The span of time measured by generations does not suffice for such primeval ages. The word *olam* appears here, corresponding to the Greek *aion*, the Latin *aevum*, the English aeon. The aeon is a cycle of time. God lives from *olam* to *olam*, from aeon to aeon, from one time-cycle to another. The Psalm says quite literally: "And from *olam* to *olam*—THOU GOD". That means the same as "thou art". Not "thou wert". Just as Christ does not say, "Before Abraham was, I was"—but, "I AM". Before Abraham entered life—I AM. That is timeless. It is removed from all sequence of time, from the state of being earlier and from the state of being later. It is above and beyond any temporal element. It has this meaning here, too, in the Psalm: "From time-cycle to time-cycle—Thou Art".

Out of this timelessness come the words of destiny which speak of man's death.

> *Thou lettest us mortals return to dust*
> *And Thou sayest, come again, ye children of men.*
> *For a thousand years in thy sight are but one day;*
> *As yesterday that has come and gone,*
> *Or as a watch in the night.*

The Psalm knows that in the higher worlds time is different from what it is on earth. There is no growing old, no being "superannuated" there, the millennia lie like an open book before the eyes of God. In contrast to the divine timelessness the transitory nature of man's earthly existence is presented in three pictures. It is like the stream that flows past, like running water that cannot be held fast. It is like sleep, for earthly human consciousness is in fact like being shrouded in darkness, like sleep in comparison with super-sensory, spiritual consciousness. It is like a flower soon faded away.

> *Thou carriest our lives away as with a flood;*
> *they are as a sleep.*
> *They are like grass which groweth up.*
> *In the morning it flourisheth and groweth up:*
> *In the evening it is cut down and withereth.*

Deep resignation speaks in these verses, resignation before the inevitability of death.

II

But the Psalm does not only give way to sadness. It asks about the wherefor of this destiny and ventures to give a clear answer to the question. The contemplation of our transitory life does not lead to a weak pessimism, but makes us face a fact which concerns the human being most deeply.

> *For we are consumed by thine anger*
> *And by thy wrath are we denied permanence.*
> *Thou hast set our iniquities before thee,*
> *Our secret sins in the light of thy countenance.*

If man were to consist only of something which has a short transitory existence and then merges again into the All—he would give no thought to it. He would pass away as a matter of course in the general passing away, without question and without trace. He realizes, however, that in the foundation of his being he is made of something which is more than transitory. He senses the futility of his existence as not a normal condition and feels himself to be exiled from his own setting and caught up in a way of existence that is really foreign to him. The Psalm does not merely bemoan an inexplicable destiny in this state of affairs, but confesses to an interpretation which includes man himself in the responsibility for it; it is a consequence of human sin. We are given over to transitory existence because we ourselves have failed. Our misdeeds stand "in the light of the divine countenance". Ancient visionary experience survives in such a phrase. We can start from an example still to be felt today; that we are ashamed of our faults before a revered person. This is an anticipation of the experiences that await us after death. In describing the difference between earthly and supersensible consciousness, Rudolf Steiner explained that on earth we always feel ourselves to be the observer. We take our existence for granted, and inspect our surroundings. It is just the contrary over there; we experience ourselves primarily as being observed. We feel how higher beings react toward us.

Modern man is inclined quickly to dismiss such an expression as "God's countenance" with the thought that it is only "anthropomorphism", which in a childishly naïve way projects human peculiarities on to the Divine. One attributes a countenance to God because one sees that man has a countenance. But the opposite is true. Man is in fact himself an image of God. His countenance, which we feel to be his most spiritual part, is only the reflection of an original experience in the higher world. The human being is only on the way to having a countenance. Thus a human element is not being transferred to God in an inadmissible or even childish way, but rather what is observed in man is a reflection of the reality in higher worlds. "The light of thy countenance." The Psalm knows of the power of light and thence also the judging power of the divine countenance. As the epitome of light it is at the same time the epitome of justice, it is the sun which "brings it to light". Because the Psalm knows this countenance it also knows sin. Sin is a religious concept. Without having a sense for the Divine one cannot know what sin is.

The visions of Moses in Genesis include the Fall and the driving out of man from Paradise into the sphere of the transitory and perishable. Why had God no choice but to make man's body die?

The earthly body is something like an insulated cell in its material density. It promotes the development of an independent ego-consciousness. This ego-consciousness in its early stages has received a self-centred egotistic character through Lucifer. The material body is the firm stronghold of this egotistic self. If transitoriness had not been implanted into this insulated earthly body man would have become immortal in his God-estranged selfhood.

As "fallen" man he would have become eternal and thereby lost to the Divine world. Thus it was a wise measure of Providence to ensure that man could only be active for a certain time in the earthly body, giving his own stamp to his personality, and that he was then recalled through death to his home in the spiritual world for a longer period, so that he might not completely lose touch with the world of his origin. Thus man alternates between lives on earth where he develops his personality between birth and death—although stamped by the effect of the Fall, and periods of dwelling in the world of his origin. In the future this influence of the Fall of man is to be overcome through Christ, the self-hood gained on earth made holy and redeemed to become the true ego which places its free personality in the service of the Divine. Then the earthly and heavenly life of man can be re-united.

But this cannot as yet be seen in the 90th Psalm with full clarity. Our earthly existence is transitory and hastens towards death. It is recognized that this is connected with the Fall, that it is a reaction, a rejoinder of God to the Fall of Man. To Old Testament understanding this rejoinder flows from the "wrath" of God. "It is Thy anger which makes us pass away."

His intermingling with the Luciferic element is the reason why man, as he has become on earth, is in conflict with the divine world. When he is called home again after an earthly life this summons leads to difficult crises in the life after death. The dead must pay for their home-coming with painful purification. When they pass over they find that with earthly attainments they do not straightway "fit" into heaven, that their presence is disturbing. Earthly man with his guilt realizes his incompatibility with the world of his origin. He experiences the wrath of God.

As Christians we may venture to say: in this divine reaction which makes man mortal, nothing less than divine Love is active which saves man from being made immortal in his sinful condition. Through catastrophes, through judgments, destruction and purification, God's love ever and again calls him home. Wrath is the form which divine Love must assume when it meets with sinning man.

The 90th Psalm sees mankind standing under wrath. At the same time this is a recognition of a history, a development. For wrath is not an original state, it is a secondary condition. There could have been no wrath at the beginning. At the beginning was Love. God created man and blessed him. The Fall into Sin put an end to this primeval state. Does this second condition remain the conclusive and final one?

However, let us return to the text of the Psalm, which at first pursues the motive of transitoriness.

> *For all our days are passed away in thy wrath:*
> *And like a sigh our years pass away.*
> *The days of our years are three score years and ten,*
> *And if by reason of strength they be four score years,*
> *Their pride is laboured and futile.*
> *For it is soon cut off, and we fly away.*

The Psalm confesses that the whole pride of these few years, the attainments which man prides himself upon, is really nothing: only toil and trouble and unhappiness.

> *Who knoweth the power of thine anger?*
> *Who stands in awe before thy wrath?*

The Psalmist feels himself to be solitary in his views and experiences. With these reflections upon God's wrath he is aware that he has expressed something that lies outside general experience. Many may have a concept of "wrath", dogmatic, abstractly acquired by study and accepted. But the Psalmist speaks from direct and shattering experience, "Who knoweth the power of thine anger?" In Rudolf Steiner's book, *A Road to Self-Knowledge*, there is a passage that can make this experience of wrath concrete to us. It refers to the crossing of the threshold of the spiritual world. "Such as the soul now is, a task lies before it which it cannot master, because in its present state it is rejected by its supersensible surroundings; the spiritual world does not wish to have it within its realm. And so the soul arrives at a feeling of being in contradiction to the supersensible world; it must say to itself: as I am now it is not possible for me to mingle with that world . . . Such an experience has something annihilating in it for the Self." Here in modern terms, without reference to old texts, the experience is described which is called in Psalm 90 the "wrath of God".

> *So teach us to number our days*
> *that we may apply our hearts unto wisdom.*

To "number" our days means that we should not only think about death, but altogether charge the hollow dream of our existence with consciousness, cultivate retrospection and memory and make ourselves clear as to where we stand. To number the days can also mean: to notice the inner quality of the different stages of life. Each stage in the course of this life of seventy years has its special spiritual possibilities. It is not only youth that has its character of "once only" and "never again". Even if it is not so evident, each section of life has it connection with God. "That our heart may gain wisdom." Wisdom of the heart will mature from such responsible communing with the years of our life.

III

The attention of the Psalm now turns to the expected salvation:

> *Bring to pass the turning, O Lord. How long will*
> *it be?*
> *And have mercy on those who serve thee*
> *And satisfy us at daybreak with thy grace,*

That we shall rejoice and be glad all our days.
Make us glad according to the days wherein thou
hast afflicted us,
And the many years wherein we have seen evil.

Wrath cannot be the final state. It is a second state, which Love assumes towards sinful man.

Now expectation turns to a third state; the restitution of harmony between God and man, the re-establishment of Love. This third condition cannot come about through man. So the hopeful soul looks with anticipation to God. He may change the situation through something quite new. Here the Psalm becomes "Messianic", although no direct reference to the Messiah is made.

The prayer for the great return is followed by the sigh, "How long?" But just as the whole Psalm shows calm endurance and manly composure, so, too, is this "How long?" where personal feeling comes for once to the surface, no wild outcry; it is spoken with an understanding patience and mature calm.

"O satisfy us at daybreak with thy grace." In the Holy Scriptures we meet again and again with the mystery of the early morning. Morning is the hour when divine grace is near. Who does not feel how the whole day can be vexatious when one has begun it with a dull, heavy, sleepy morning. The Resurrection of Christ was accomplished in the early morning, still in the sphere of the night's mystery, but in the light of the dawning day. Easter is a morning event. This morning character of Christianity is significant. A new Cosmic Day begins with the Resurrection. A new ascent is established. To use the expression of Novalis, Easter is a "Festival of Cosmic Rejuvenation".

When the Mohammedan prays he turns towards Mecca. In the same way the prayers of the Psalms turn inwardly towards the approaching Christ.

A quotation from Psalm 5, 3 is specially instructive: "At daybreak I will prepare it for thee and look out for thee." The phrase "prepare it" refers to the preparation of the sacrifice, but implies at the same time an inner preparation, which enables the worshipper to open his spiritual eye during the ritual of sacrifice. "At daybreak I will prepare (it) for thee and look out for thee."

In the Psalm of Moses, the reference to "daybreak" is particularly moving. The Psalmist is the aged man, the one who has matured and grown wise. But the secret of rejuvenation, the grace of the morning, which brings about the great change, are touched upon in the last verses. They pass over from the realm of truth to a premonition of Grace. If hitherto a calm, earnest mood of grief prevailed in the Psalm, out of this very earnestness an anticipation of real joy now emerges. The wisdom of age is crystallized pain. Anticipation of redemptive grace and mercy is joy. "We shall rejoice and be glad all our days." This joy is to be a kind of compensation for the previous sorrows.

> Let thy work appear unto thy servants
> And thy glory unto their children.

This is now a prayer for the Deed of Christ. And even now that this Deed belongs to history, the petition in the Psalm has not lost its validity, for now this work should appear ever more clearly before man's perception and understanding. That the splendour of majesty should become visible "unto their children" points to a still more distant future, to the vision of the Coming of Christ in the glory of etheric light.

> And let the beauty of the Lord our God be upon
> us,
> And establish thou the work of our hands upon us;
> Yea, the work of our hands, establish thou it.

The Psalm concludes with a reference to the work of our hands. Is that not contradictory after the reflections on our transitory nature? For if everything earthly bears within it the germ of delay, is not then all activity, all working and creating, all labour of love wasted from the outset? Did it not say earlier, "As the flower blooms in the morning and at evening withers away?" It is only possible to understand the remarkable change to a positive mood when one takes the "great turning" seriously. It is true that it is only being prayed for. But it seems as if something of its nature had already been imparted in advance to him who prays. The morning light of Easter radiates over the close of this Psalm of Moses.

The closing lines of the Psalm underscore this positive affirmation of life which calls all good forces into action: "Yea, the work of our hands, establish Thou it." The Hebrew does not really say "establish" but "confirm", "sanction". In the light of the Resurrection our own works acquire eternal significance. They become confirmed, "established" through a divine "Yea, so be it".

The Psalm sees together the eternity of God and the fate of mortal man. But in prophetic vision it anticipates the coming salvation which will unite the two, by God's grace, and thereby give meaning to man's life and work on earth.

In Exile

PSALMS 42 AND 43

I

The two Psalms 42 and 43 are intimately connected. Together
they form a whole, as one can see from the recurring verses 42;
6 and 11, and 43; 5. Considered historically, it is the Psalm of a
priest apparently banished from Jerusalem and living in exile in
the region of the source of the Jordan. It expresses his longing for
the Temple worship in Jerusalem. But the Psalm expresses truths
which hold good far beyond this special situation of a long past
destiny.

I

As the hart panteth after the water brooks
So panteth my soul after Thee, O God.
My soul thirsteth for God, for the living God;
When shall I come and see the face of God?
My tears have been my meat day and night,
While they continually say unto me,
    Where is thy God?
I shall remember these things and pour out my
    soul in remembering them.
I had gone with the multitude, and went with
    them to the house of God,
With the voice of joy and praise, with the
    multitude that kept the Festival.
Why art thou cast down, O my soul, and why
    art thou restless within me?

*Hope thou in God: for I shall yet praise him
that he is the help of my countenance and
my God.*

The opening words are famous. It is the picture of the stag
which seeks in vain for water in the dried-up brook under the
baking heat of the sun. The elemental power of this natural
picture has been felt through the ages.

Desires, pleasures, pains, meet us in the animal kingdom with
undiminished power. The animal merges completely with its
emotions, tastes them to the uttermost. With man, the development of the intellect has "sicklied o'er with the pale cast of
thought" the naturally powerful colour of these feelings and
paralysed them. The cry of an animal can "go through and
through" us, and we can learn from it what a passionate emotion
can be. Human passions seem tame and insignificant compared
with such elemental outbursts.

However, this was different in past ages. When the Iliad describes the terrible wrath of Achilles in the image of a spreading
forest fire, we get some inkling of the strength of human emotions in ancient times. However, man is not condemned perma-
nently to pay for his clear consciousness by stunting the soul. This
is only a transitional stage. He may be tempted by a false path
to revive the full gamut of passions and emotions by reverting
to the animal or even the demon in him. On the other hand, a
healthy future possibility awaits him. Powerful and exciting
sensations will open up in him, in the same measure as he makes
an active and conscious contact with the world of Spirit. These
sensations are no longer fettered to the darkness of his animal
nature, but are in harmony with the consciousness of vision. The
soul feels with the spirit. It is only in the form of the intellect
that spirit is an adversary of the soul.

The Apocalypse of St. John describes the Cherubim in the
form of living beasts who sound forth the great song of praise.
These celestial creatures are "full of eyes before and behind".
No dull blindness of instinct is seeking an outlet, but eye-faculties

4

of the highest order are in action. Here the elemental power of passion is spiritualized, not deadened, but dedicated with all its strength to the spirit.

The cry of the animal is on the one hand a reminder to man of a lost power of soul. On the other hand it is a prophecy that the human soul will one day again soar aloft on the wings of powerful emotions which are stirred by the spirit.

Thus a religious man sees again in the panting of the hart his own longing. Thirst is in fact one of the most powerful sensations. It serves as a classical symbol of human desire, particularly in Buddhism. Buddha saw in thirst the burning subconscious longing for life and existence, which leads us again and again into the body, and hence again and again into suffering. He saw no other way of ending this suffering than to penetrate in meditation into the subconscious depths of the soul and destroy there at the roots this urge for existence.

It has only been recognized since the coming of Christ that in spite of its sufferings earthly existence must not be regarded merely negatively. Since that time we must not see the path to incarnation as a false path. The burning thirst which leads to earthly existence has its justification, but it must be rightly understood. We must recognize whence this thirst, this longing for existence, is ultimately directed; it must not be content with temporary and superficial appeasements. This thirst for existence that guides us with a deep instinct into our earthly life is, after all, the longing of man for his self-realization, the longing to grasp his destiny and to become the bearer of the I AM. This longing is at the same time the desire for the God of the I AM, who, as the creative prototype of true Egohood within us, will bring about the realization of our Self. Ultimately this thirst is seeking Christ. It leads us to earthly existence because it is only on earth that we can really find the Christ in His Death and Resurrection; without Him earthly existence and the thirst for it would be meaningless.

Thirst is also referred to in St. John's Gospel when Christ cries from the Cross, "I thirst". It is as though with this cry He

took into His divine soul the totality of the pain of human longing in order that He might fully identify Himself with humanity.
But by doing so He can give man the promise: "He that believeth
on me shall never thirst". (St. John 6; 35, also 4, 14 and 7; 37).

Let us turn back to our Psalm, from which we seem to have
wandered a long way, but in order really to see it in this great
context.

"My soul thirsteth for God, for the living God." Here the
primal emotion of thirst has become conscious of its true object.
Unhappily, the expression "the living God" has largely become
religious jargon. The "living" God is the God acting directly and
spontaneously, not only working in the law, in the impersonal
necessity of what He has ordained. When creation was complete
the great Sabbath rest began: God has ceased to create. Creation
now runs along its own rails, as it were. But where behind the
world which gradually became more a concealment than a revelation is the God who acts spontaneously, who once commanded,
"Let there be light!"?

The Christ brought the great Sabbath to an end. A renewal of
the original powers of creation is accomplished in Him. The
world has detached itself to a certain degree from the creator
and has become "finished work". But the creativity of God
appears again in the I AM of the Christ. He who utters the "I
AM" is the "living God".

"When shall I come and see the face of God?" A long path of
development leads to this seeing. At some future time we shall
stand before God as ego to Ego, spirit-personality to spirit-personality. As St. Paul says, "But then face to face".

The striving soul must for a time endure mockery, for the
adversaries ask, "Where is now thy God?" The man who is
called to freedom must at some time have his relation to God
exposed to the test of persecution, to prove that it is sustained
purely inwardly, without external props and support. The scorn
of the adversaries who only have eyes for the material world and
who, through what they find, come to the conclusion that there
is no God—that is something that had of necessity to arise in the

course of time. It is a station on the way of the Cross, of the God who gave up His power for the sake of our freedom. Atheism is no accidental going off the rails, no product of special wickedness, but something that had to come for a time. The suffering of the Psalmist is not only his fortuitous personal misfortune but a share of the great divine-human Passion.

Memories arise in this state of forlornness—"I had it once". The Psalmist is speaking of his memories of the Temple worship in Jerusalem, of solemn celebrations in the sanctuary which in those days mediated to him a consciousness of God. He speaks for mankind in general. Up till now Religion has largely lived by reason of such memories of a past nearness of God. The writer of our Psalm pours out his soul in remembrance. He gathers all the energies of his soul into this remembering and turns it into a meditation.

We must adopt again the right technique of remembering. In the course of our life we shall all have had many more impressions of a higher reality than may perhaps appear to us today. We go about with our experiences for the most part like thoughtless spendthrifts. We could derive more from the fact that this or that has befallen us. "I will remember these things and pour out my soul in remembering them."

The first section of the Psalm ends with the verse which then recurs after the second and third section: "Why art thou cast down, O my soul? Why are thou restless within me?" It is part of an active religion that one is no longer so inevitably absorbed in one's pains and griefs. One divides oneself, so to speak, into the person who suffers and the one who stands by. This other one who stands by is often still very feeble; sometimes he stands perhaps "wringing his hands" before his own soul when it withdraws from his encouragement. But again and again the attempt must be made to take up a position outside oneself and from this objective standpoint to call one's soul to order.

The Psalmist places himself similarly before his own soul, which is utterly lost in grief and cannot find its way to inner peace and calm. He offers comfort to his soul, "Hope thou in God". After each of the three stanzas the encouragement is repeated. The soul is not so quickly freed from its sorrow and restlessness; for at the beginning of the second section this reference to being cast down is brought up again, "My soul is cast down within me", as if there had been no exhortation to courage. But repetition is the secret of the inner life. So the Psalm again and again places spiritual comfort before the mind's eye, until it really takes root in the soul.

II

My soul is cast down within me:
Therefore will I remember thee in the land of
    Jordan, and of Hermon, high on Mount Misar.
Deep calleth unto deep at the roar of thy brooks.
All thy waves and thy billows have gone over me.
Yet the Lord will command his loving kindness
    in the daytime
And in the night his song shall be within me,
A prayer unto the living God.

The Psalmist, banished from Jerusalem, lives in exile by the upper waters of the Jordan, which dash in tumbling waterfalls from the mountains near to snow-covered Hermon. In this region, encompassed by elemental forces, a famous sanctuary was dedicated to Pan near Baneas, the later Caesarea-Philippi. In the future Peter was here to make his avowal, "Thou art the Christ, the son of the living God". (Matt. 16; 16.)

The Psalmist sees himself abandoned to the roaring waterfalls, as if the ancient dragon-power of chaos had risen up—*Thehom*—the primal flood, not yet subdued by the Ego-God—*abyssos* in the Greek translation. It has a hidden connection with the chaotic powers within him, with the inner restlessness of his soul, surging and storming without peace, which he is not able at once to control. It is as if all these waves were dashing together above his head, passing lightly over his painstaking attempts to take hold of himself.

The pain of exile has gripped him with all its force. Exile—it has been experienced and suffered a millionfold in our own time; torn away from house and home, from the familiar cherished surroundings, uprooted from one's work and profession—this being dispossessed and exiled into a strange land, hostile and cold.

But with all its hardships being exiled is also a parable of higher things. Opening our eyes in the morning in strange surroundings, have we not at times felt that this condition is known and familiar? As if one had gone through this nightmare of waking in exile in some other form? To awake in a foreign land of exile—this is the archetypal experience of incarnation, of embodiment on earth. Our soul has been displaced from its own original environment and banished into an environment not fitted for it, into the world of material things. This transplanting from the heavenly home into the material world is the archetypal experience of exile, which still trembles in the depths of every soul. The religious sense is an awakening homesickness, a dark recollection of a "beforehand". Religion loses this character of looking back to the past only by the acceptance of the Christ, because through Christ the heavenly home can be carried into earthly exile, transforming all things.

The nightly song of praise, the prayer of which the following verse speaks, are the effort to meet the chaotic mood of mourning and unrest and to make way again for the rule of the ego. It would not be right merely to say, "I am not in the mood to pray—it cannot be expected of me today". We must get away from this subjective mood of up and down. Prayer does not grow from moods, but the true mood comes out of the prayer. Here regular rhythmical repetition is a help. The regular celebration of the Festivals in the Act of Consecration of Man throughout the year is something quite independent of the moods that are produced by the changing destinies of individuals. It takes hold of man and comforts him and takes him into a larger, more expansive life.

The blessing rests with God; man's efforts may for a time seem
to bear no fruit. But a healing element lies in the very effort of
observing regular ordered prayer.

So the Psalmist sings his nocturnal hymn. He does not admit
that pain uses up all the energy of his soul and makes it completely "toneless". There must always be something left over
which is capable of exaltation. To take part in the times and
rhythms of an ordered religious life is a great help.

The Psalm carries its afflictions before the Godhead:

> I will say unto God, my rock, why hast thou forgotten
> me?
> Why go I mourning because of the mockery of the
> enemy?
> As with a sword in my bones, my enemies reproach me;
> While they say daily unto me, "Where is thy God?"

My "rock"—the antithesis to the chaotic flood of *thehom*. The
rock, the ego-foundation, the solid ground under the feet that
allows us to stand and withstand. This power proceeds from the
God of the I AM.

"Why hast thou forgotten me?" The human being is set free
by the higher powers. They have renounced the task of guiding
him step by step. They have untied the string. He is to seek his
way on his own responsibility. We cannot be spared this experience of being "forsaken by God". It makes us mature enough to
find in freedom our helper and guide in Christ.

The question, "Where is thy God?" is an added affliction in
this forsaken state. In the first part it was the cause of tears; now
it is enhanced: it is "like a sword in my bones". The pain produced by the thought that in this earthly sphere the divine can
be "called in question" goes through bone and marrow.

So now for the second time the consolation of the spirit is
invoked:

> Why art thou cast down, O my soul? Why art
> thou restless within me?

Hope thou in God; for I shall yet praise him,
Who is the health of my countenance and my
comfort.

We must summon ourselves to hope, in the consciousness that we are involved in far-reaching developments, in great plans of Providence which we are as yet quite unable to survey. We need to be conscious of the fact that we are in a lengthy process of becoming, which takes its time. We need the "long will" which leads through the various phases of becoming with their inevitable sorrows and suffering. Such a "long will" produces then the right kind of patience, not a passive mood of letting things happen, but a positive attitude of mind.

"I shall yet praise him who is the health of my countenance", as the One who helps me to my true human countenance, whereas evil "disfigures" it. As the One who brings the human countenance into reality, He is "my God", the God of my ego, who is revealed in the free personality, in the true nature of the human being.

III

Judge me, O God, and plead my cause against an
ungodly nation:
O deliver me from the deceitful and wicked man!

The God who will help us towards our true human countenance is at the same time the Judge who brings to our consciousness our disfigurements and inhumanities. This judgment, however, aims not at condemnation but at restoration.

Inasmuch as we deliver ourselves to the judgment of the ego-creating God—"Judge me, O God"—we gain in God the helper against our opponents. He who shrinks from the divine judgment of conscience falls of necessity into the hands of the evil powers. To become honestly conscious of our faults separates us from the devil. Inward dishonesty that tries to drown conscience leads us all the more definitely into his realm. The human enemies mentioned in the Psalm are only the visible representatives of the invisible powers, of "ungodliness" and "deceit" and of "wickedness". God Himself wages war against these powers, if we do not withdraw ourselves from His judgment. Then God becomes our confederate, inasmuch as He fights our battles and takes from us the power of the Adversary, as we hear in the Act of Consecration of Man.

> *For thou art the God of my strength:*
> *Why hast thou cast me off?*
> *Why must I go mourning*
> *Because of the mockery of the enemy?*

The question, "Why hast thou forgotten me?" is here intensified to the still more forcible, "Why hast thou cast me off?" Possibilities of fearful catastrophe appear on the horizon with these questions. Since man's own freedom, his good will, is counted upon in the process of his becoming true man, since he must himself bring into operation through his positive attitude the grace that is destined for him, it is possible for this development to be wrecked by his own unwillingness to co-operate. Then he would be abandoned as an unfinished attempt. "Unfit for becoming Man." The Psalmist feels himself to be "one of the damned", he feels as if he were in an inferno. Yet he lifts his soul again to the prospect of divine grace.

> *O send out thy light and thy truth:*
> *They will lead me and bring me unto thy holy hill,*
> *And thy tabernacles.*
> *Then will I go to the altar of God.*
> *Unto God who is my exceeding joy:*
> *Yea, upon the harp will I praise thee,*
> *O God, Who is the God of my I.*

Deliverance comes because God sends down to us something of His own being. It is like an emanation, an outflow of the divine essence in the direction of man. "Thy light and thy truth." Both

4*

words appear in the I AM words of St. John's Gospel where Christ declares the nature of his own being. "I AM the light of the world." "I AM the way, the truth and the life."

These divine essential forces "will accompany me and will make me come (literally) to the hill of thy holiness." This accompanying is in no way a carrying, but it presupposes the participation of man's own forces for progress.

The attainment of the goal, the bringing home of the exiled sufferer from the strange land to the centre of divine life is presented in three stages. The holy mountain, the tabernacles of God, His altar. The holy mountain is in general the figurative expression for exaltation into a "higher" world. It begins with the raising of fallen man to the mountain-high world of divine holiness. If a man has climbed the holy hill, he finds there the "tabernacles of God". Is a picture of the "dwelling place" only a childish way of carrying earthly things into the divine realm? Again the reverse is true: our dwelling at a particular place is only an earthly image of the fact that the higher world too, although non-spatial, has differing realms and regions. "In my Father's house are many mansions." "Thy dwellings" (plural in the original) are the various realms forming the home of the Higher Beings in their infinitely rich and manifold differentiation, in whom God reveals Himself in countless ways. In this way they are dwelling places of God.

Finally, the third and last state is in the heart of heaven, the inmost centre of the divine world, the Altar of God, where His own love-offering is fulfilled, the imparting of His own being. All earthly altars are symbols of this mystery of the divine sacrifice. Man is called upon to participate in the divine cosmic service of sacrifice. As man he is called to the priesthood. "And I will approach the altar of God." He takes this step from the prompting of his inmost being. Then the divine leaders, light and truth, are no longer merely beside him, giving help and guidance, it is as though they have entered into him and taken part in his own decision. So that, notwithstanding all the gracious help given to him, to approach this altar is ultimately man's own free act.

To participate thus in the divine cosmic service of sacrifice is at the same time the highest blessedness—"To the God who is my joy and my delight." Man who has received through aeons the divine sacrificial gifts, now becomes a being who himself may give, may sacrifice, thus giving back in changed form to the world what he has received. "It is more blessed to give than to receive." This, speaking broadly, is the ultimate purpose of the whole of human evolution. The "heavenly bliss" of man does not consist in the indolent enjoyment of a sort of Utopia, but in being permitted to share in the creative sacrificial deeds of God.

"Yea, upon the harp will I praise thee." The human being has now become "resounding", all the false notes and dissonances of his nature are overcome; he is a walking song of praise. Our soul-life always resounds in some way in the higher worlds, seldom harmoniously, generally quite the opposite. The Christ-filled man must develop his soul with all its powers of resonance to become the harp of God. Thus the Apocalypse of St. John sees the redeemed as playing on the harp (Rev. 14; 2).

This reference to approaching the altar of God is like an apocalyptic vision of the future. But now the Psalm leaves this vision of the future to the present, and at last to exorcize the despair and unrest of his suffering soul through words of spiritual consolation:

> Why art thou cast down, O my soul, and art
> so restless within me?
> Hope thou in God, for yet will I thank him
> that he is the help of my countenance and
> my God.

A Glimpse into the Sanctuary

PSALM 73

I

"Nevertheless, I am continually with thee. Thou holdest me by my right hand. Thou guidest me with thy counsel and at last receivest me with honour. Whom have I in heaven but Thee? And there is none upon earth that I desire beside Thee. If my flesh and my soul languish, yet thou, O God, art the comfort of my heart and my portion for ever."

These verses (73 ; 23–26) have always been regarded as one of the finest passages of the Old Testament, in fact of the religious literature of all time. One must see them in connection with the entire Psalm in order to give them their full value.

The writer of the Psalm tells us at first how for a long time he was oppressed by a tormenting problem. His difficult destiny led him to the question: How is it that evil is so often successful, that so little of the divine justice appears? And on the other hand, so often the life of a man who endeavours with all his power to do what is right seems insignificant and beset with trouble.

The first sixteen verses are devoted to the presentation of this problem. They describe in vivid and picturesque language the triumph of those who do not trouble about godly things, and then in contrast to this his own sorrowful, afflicted life.

However much I pondered to understand this,
it was too painful for me. (v. 16).

He sometimes felt tempted to doubt the existence of divine

justice, but something always held him back. Until one day something unusual happened to him. His honest efforts towards understanding, his steady endurance of physical pain (v. 14) his struggle for purity and holiness (v. 13) and assuredly also the fact that he belonged to the community of the "Sons of God"—all this had made him mature enough for "initiation".

Until I entered into the sanctuaries of God.

This verse 17 is the decisive passage in the 73rd Psalm. Biblical criticism has puzzled a good deal over it. Scholars have wondered about the plural, "the sanctuaries" of God, which would imply that it was not the Temple which was meant. And yet it could only refer to the Temple? It is our belief that the sentence becomes comprehensible when one assumes a supersensible experience. One can understand "the entry into the sanctuaries of God" only as one of those events where the "wall" of the material world seems to open, and behind it a world is revealed which previously had been completely outside our consciousness. A world,—indeed, worlds of divine life in various ranks and stages—"the sanctuaries of God". Actual entry into the Temple and observation of the sacrificial ritual may have brought about this supersensible experience. The Psalms occasionally point to this power of ritual to release supersensible vision; for the Temple is the place "where thine honour dwells", thy *gloria*, thy revelation of light.

A new light has been shed on the problems and questions of the one so sorely tried. He has a glimpse of things to come. He sees through the transitory nature of earthly existence. A life whose external conditions are fortunate and happy now becomes unimportant for him in view of the outcome. That an evil earthly life peters out into emptiness is henceforth deeply known by him.

As a dream whose vanity we know when we awake. (v. 20).

Even the word "awake" possesses here the peculiar colour of mystical experience. The earthly life formerly accepted as final, and taken seriously in a false way, is felt to be a dream from which one awakes into a real world. Without doubt, in the same mystical context of an awakening to higher consciousness the same expression occurs in the significant sentence of the 17th Psalm: "I will behold thy face in righteousness. I shall be satisfied when I awake with thy likeness". (17; 15.) Even beyond the beholding of God's face the intuitive perception of the "likeness" of God leads here to a being fed supernaturally, to a communion. The rare word used here means the essential form, as it were the "ego-contour" of God, to behold which, according to Numbers 12; 8, was permitted to Moses alone. Only a most sublime "awakening" can lead to such an experience.

After this awakening—to turn back again now to Psalm 73—man looks back at his earthly being as it has been hitherto, seeing it from outside and feeling deeply impressed with its incompatibility. "I was a fool without knowledge, a beast was I before thee." (v. 22.) It now becomes clear to the Psalmist that his earlier, earthbound efforts to think remained powerless to grasp divine reality. He looks back at his unitiated human state as something still subhuman, like an animal.

Only now the Psalm rises to the heights of the words quoted at the beginning. If we reproduce the Hebrew text now with our fresh understanding, it reads somewhat as follows:

> *My ego—for ever with thee!*
> *My right hand hast thou grasped.*
> *Thou guidest me by thy counsel.*
> *And one day thou takest me into thy glory.*
> *Who else in the heavens is the creative archetype of my*
>   *ego-being?*
> *And united with thee I confront what is earthly in freedom.*
> *Then may my body pass away,*
> *My soul pass away also.*
> *For evermore is God the rock-foundation of my heart and*
>   *my destiny.*   (v. 23–26.)

These verses are so unusual because they are the fruit of an initiation, a gift from the world of the "divine sanctuaries".

The sentence, "A beast was I before thee" had preceded them.

Now the Psalmist feels himself for the first time in his true Ego, as a real human being. He knows that his true Ego is henceforth united indissolubly with God. "And my Ego—evermore it is with thee." This union with God is demonstrated in three stages. They are: the hand-clasp, wise guidance, fulfilment.

The hand-clasp: there are Egyptian figures of the Sun-God, where the rays of the sun terminate in hands. In this reference to the divine hand which grasps our hand one should not see a primitive "anthropomorphism" but rather consider that man, on his side, is "theomorphic", that divine secrets are revealed in his form. This is especially the case in the marvel of the human hand. That God grasps our right hand is not accidental. We are more conscious and awake on the right side than on the left. We must find contact with God through our conscious personality.

Guidance: that grasping of the hand issues into wise guidance. The Psalmist is no longer restless about his difficult destiny. An initiation does not mean that the path of life ceases to be thorny, but we can now see it in another light. The initiate trusts in the divine guidance which has led him to his destiny with a wisdom that surpasses all human understanding.

Fulfilment: the distant aim is seen from afar—"some day"— "at last". The original text here speaks quite simply and concisely of a "taking"—"thou takest me". To take—this is used in the same sense in the short oracular sentence in Genesis about Enoch (Gen. 5; 24). Since he walked "with God", God "took" him.

God released man once from His own original substance and set him free to lead an independent life. But this releasing and setting free is for the sake of union again at a higher stage. Man must so shape his freedom that one day he stands with his independence not without but within the Godhead. God lets man go free in order to take him back again in love into His kingdom. When some day in the far future man will be utterly permeated with Christ, then in his whole being of spirit, soul and body he will be "membered" into the heavens. This ascent into heaven was prophetically prefigured in the far past in the future of Enoch. In monumental words Genesis says of him that God "took" him.

There is not only the Communion in which we take God into ourselves, but some day when evolution has come to an end there is to be a communion in which man will be received into God. This will come about when man has utterly and entirely become ripe for eternity, when he can be received by the world of his origin without loss of substance through the survival of earthly remainders and residue. What the 73rd Psalm expresses as a kind of presentiment is this great "reception" that awaits man. "In glory" does not mean only with honour, but the Hebrew *kābôd* points to the *gloria*, the light of transfiguration into which man enters when he is received.*

Psalm 49; 14, 15 is another parallel. First comes the impressive description of the godless in *Sheol*, in the world of the shades (*Hades* for the Greeks). "Death tends them". In contrast to this the Psalm is assuring: "Yet God will deliver my soul from the hand of *Sheol;* for he will take me". Apart from Psalm 16, which we shall still consider (page 124), Psalm 73; 24 and Psalm 49; 16 are the only passages in the Psalter which venture to say with such boldness that man shall be preserved throughout eternity.

The words, "Whom have I in heaven but thee? And there is none upon earth that I desire beside Thee", are slightly different in the original Hebrew. They read, literally, "who to me in the Heavens?" The human being finds himself in the higher world, looks round on all sides and seeks among the hosts of spirits and their spheres for his special spiritual home. There in the higher worlds in creative activity the divine archetypes of the crystals, the plants, the animals are to be found. But where does the human being find the region which for him as man has a corresponding archetypal significance? Where is his own, his human heavenly prototype? "Who to me in the heavens?" The dative "to me" points simply and expressively to the nature of this divine Being who is sought by man and who is inclined to him and allied with him. So we can translate it, "Who else but thee, the God of my I AM, is the creative archetype of my human nature?".

"When I am united with thee I have no pleasure in earthly

* As already explained in chapter 1 and others.

things." I am no longer dependent on the terrestrial, I feel myself sovereign above earthly things. Man is then no longer bound to the earth through possession and desire, he faces the earth freely as a king.

To have become independent of earthly things leads the Psalmist out of the problem which embittered his former life when he still took the perishable world for the final reality and was a "beast before God". The freedom which has been gained is shown in the cry, "and even if my body and soul should pass away!" Inner ascendancy lies in this "even if". Linked with the God of his humanity he can look calmly on the passing away of his earthly bodily nature.

But we are concerned here not only with the "flesh" but also with the soul; in the original text, "heart". The following line, however, shows that the heart that "passes away" is not the inmost core of man's being. "Thou art the comfort of my heart for ever." Only the mortal heart passes away and the life of the soul in so far as it is bound to the earthly body and is affected by the ups and downs of the bodily nature. The soul life bound to the transitory body will pass and its passing away should be borne with equanimity. The Psalmist knows through his awakening that our relation to God must be anchored much deeper than in the fluctuating and changing of our daily emotions. There is a more solid anchor, independent of recurring moods. There are situations in life where a man "loses his nerve", where his emotional life is overwhelmed by catastrophic events. As Psalm 42 suggested to us, a man must be able to stand outside these moods, these doubts and depressions, at least with part of his self. If he has found this "outside" basis he knows that though perhaps he cannot always be immediately successful, he is nevertheless on the way to control his disturbed emotions. The transitory nature of our body, its becoming ill and old, and hence, too, the transitory nature of a considerable part of our feelings, must all be regarded with tranquillity, in view of man's eternal significance.

In spite of his great experience of God, the Psalmist realizes that he must yet pass through deep waters. But he is no longer fettered to the world of appearances. "God is the rock of my heart and my portion in eternity". Here the "heart" is not the transitory seat of passing emotions but the immortal heart, through whose powers of faith man finds his firm foundation on the eternal rock of God. "And my portion"—the allotted share of man's life is to be God Himself. One who can speak like this has become free of fears and anxieties, heedless of whether he has his due share of earthly life, of whether life allots him the amount of good fortune, comfort and satisfaction that he thinks he is entitled to have. In the past God said to Abraham, "I myself am thy exceeding great reward". Ultimately the value of life consists in the "divine portion" which we carry away as our life's fruit. Anything else, joys or sorrows, pass away.

Finally, of all the problems there remains for the Psalm only this one alternative—nearness to God or distance from God.

> For lo, they that are far from thee perish.
> Thou givest to non-existence him who breaks the
>   covenant with thee. (v. 27.)

Here is no revengeful act of an offended God, rather a kind of higher law of nature taking effect. He who gives up his relation to God delivers himself up of his own accord to a condition of nothingness.

> And I—the nearness of God is my good. (v. 28.)

The nearness of God is "the" good, the value of values.

In this concluding verse 28 there occurs for the first and only time in this Psalm the name of Jahve, intensified still more by the addition of adon, Lord.

> I have taken my refuge with the Kyrios, the God of the I AM

Who belongs to me in the heavens? Where is the divine background whence the true being of man can proceed? The adon Jahve, the Kyrios, the God of the I AM, in truth is the God of Man.

The Passion Psalm of the Redeemer

PSALM 22

"My God, my God, why hast thou forsaken me?" With this cry, tragically familiar from the story of the Passion, the 22nd Psalm begins in the depths of desolation. But it leads in the end to a glory all the more radiant. The Psalm not only embraces Death, but also Resurrection and Glorification.

The religious experience of a devout man of the Old Testament has been carried to such depths that it becomes archetypal. Christianity has always rightly regarded this Psalm as an inspired anticipation of the Passion and the Glorification of Christ.

I

My God, my God, why hast Thou forsaken me?
Far removed is what would heal me.
Loudly I call, but I cannot reach it.
Thou God from Whom I have come,
I call to Thee in the day time
But Thou dost not answer,
And in the night season I find no rest.

He who voices this cry feels the existence of God most strongly. He senses His reality not only as that of a universal God, but as of a Being deeply belonging to himself: "My God"; or "Thou Being of God in Whom my Ego-Being rests". But the original and natural intimate personal relationship has been lost. The soul faces an incomprehensible separation from this divine Being to

Whom it belongs. Without the familiar presence which in the past has been around and above him, the human being feels painfully incomplete. Left to himself he tastes bitter loneliness.

In modern times we have become accustomed to this loneliness. We accept it almost as a natural condition. We know no better. We fail to realize that our loneliness is due to being cut off from something higher which really belongs to us. So we begin to question the meaning of life. It appears senseless. At the bottom of this is a sense of loss; but no-one knows what is actually lost. The Psalmist, however, does know. But he is faced with the mysterious fact that this higher Being Who sends His rays from above into the soul, and Who gives fullness and depth to human life, can no longer be felt as present with him.

Try as he will, he can no longer re-establish the broken link. His cry no longer penetrates; the distance has become too great. All the same, the cry uttered from the depths of his heart is not entirely in vain. Although it cannot bridge the gulf it does recall the reassuring memory: "It has not always been like this. The Divine had not yet vanished from amongst our ancestors." All myths and sacred stories of a better, golden past witness to the original community between God and Man. The Psalmist recalls first his own ancestors. But they are at the same time the link with that universal past. The comforting picture of the ancient community of worshippers, with whom the Godhead communicated in real presence stands before his mind's eye. When the sacred hymns of old were chanted, the sounds formed a throne for God.

> Thou art there, none the less, Thou Holy One,
> Descending upon the hymns of Israel.
> Our fathers trusted in Thee.
> They trusted and Thou didst help them.
> They cried to Thee, and rescue came.
> They had faith and were not disappointed.

II

However, this memory of the past provides only passing comfort. The glories of history are very little help in the present distress. A strident discord breaks through the echo of the ancient hymns: "But I!" In contrast to these past times the pain of being left alone on the earth is felt all the more poignantly. The over-shadowing Ego of God has withdrawn beyond reach. And since man is no longer sustained from above, he is in danger of drifting into the sub-human. His very Being is threatened. While the body still preserves its noble form, the inner man which ensouls this body fails to maintain true humanity. As Mephistopheles says when Faust dies, "Here is the little soul, Psyche with her wings—rip out the wings and an ugly worm is left."

> *But I!—a worm, no man.*
> *A caricature, despised and mocked.*

The terror caused by the distorted picture of Man turns into an experience of being mocked. Very likely the Psalmist remembers the sneer of actual enemies. But these adversaries who hate him become a parable. So does he who is mocked. He is no longer just anybody who has enemies; he is Archetypal Man. The adversaries are the powers of evil, trying with satanic frenzy to tread underfoot the divine image of Man. They are bent upon destroying the life-work of the Gods: Man. And since Man has succumbed to the Fall, there is no lack of points of attack, nor of causes for hellish triumphs.

> *All who see me, despise me,*
> *Shaking their heads and*
> *Mouthing insults:*
> *'Let him cast his misery upon the Lord.*
> *Maybe he will save Him*
> *If He delights in him.'*

The report of the Passion in the Gospel of St. Matthew contains literal references to these lines. But it is rather primitive to think that St. Matthew has simply taken over his report from this Psalm. On the contrary the Psalm is an anticipation and pre-vision of Golgotha, when Christ in His mercy will unite Him-self with the earthly being of Man, and surrender Himself to the derision and mockery of His adversaries. No doubt the style of St. Matthew has been influenced by the Psalm, but in reality the Psalm anticipated the future act of Golgotha.

This second wave of pain is stilled not by help from the dis-tant past, but by a recollection of childhood. Each human being is still carried at the beginning of his earthly life by the powers of God, just as humanity as a whole was borne in the arms of God at the beginning of Creation. In the womb and at his mother's breast the child is still deeply linked in complete naturalness with the divine forces of Life.

> *What hand but Thine drew me out*
> *From my mother's womb?*
> *Who else was my refuge when I hung*
> *Upon my mother's breast?*
> *From the hour of my birth I was thrown upon Thee,*
> *From my mother's womb Thou art my God.*

III

However, even this comfort which comes from the recollection of childhood is not equal to the heavy burden which is still to be put upon Man. A third wave of pain approaches. It rises still higher than those which have gone before. It carries pain to the utmost extremity—and thereby leads to the great turning point.

> *Do not place distance between Thee and me.*
> *For anguish closes in*
> *And there is none to help me.*
> *Big bulls are all around me.*
> *Strong bulls are closing in.*

Lions with gaping jaws
Are roaring for their prey.

The "anguish" announces a new terror. The forms of wild animals which assail Man are nightmarish visions. They are not the Bull and Lion of the vision of Ezekiel, belonging to the realm of the Cherubim. They are caricatures, distorted reflections in the nether world. In the vision of Ezekiel Bull and Lion are servants of the Son of God and carry His Throne. Here in the Psalm they are pictures of the forces of the soul which cut themselves off in egocentric isolation. They do not serve a Higher Being; they turn against Man with intent to destroy him.

From the picture of soul forces turning into beasts, the Psalm proceeds to the region of the etheric forces of life. These too are affected by destruction. "The Water of Life" has run dry in the human being deserted by God. The material body is no longer adequately sustained by the forces of Life. It dries up and crumbles. The bones which in the course of evolution have gradually solidified out of the fluid and quickening substance of life, are used as a picture to describe the dead substances which fall as sediment out of the original totality of life, and become subject to gravity. "All my bones are out of joint." The earthly body, seized by the Powers of Death, deserted by life, drops away as a corpse and disintegrates.

I am spent as spilt water.
All my bones are out of joint.
My heart has turned to molten wax within me.
My strength is dried up like parched clay,
My tongue sticks fast in my mouth.
Through Thee I am reduced to the dust of death.

The sensation of dying is followed by horrible spectres which rise from the Underworld. Hades, the valley of the shadow of death, approaches in the picture of a pack of attacking hounds. Orientals are familiar with the sight of wild dogs falling upon a carcass. Here they become the image of the forces of the Under-world which threaten those souls after death which have lost their divine nature. "The Hound of Hell" in the myth of Hercules is a reality.

The sufferer sees his hands and feet transfixed. He "can count all his bones". He perceives himself crucified. It was a hasty con-clusion on the part of certain theological critics when they tried to explain the wounds of Christ in terms of the 22nd Psalm. The Psalmist felt the Stigmata in his own hands and feet and his personal suffering became a prophetic eye which beheld the future Passion of the Redeemer. Christ suffered the Stigmata in historical reality, as the whole Passion of Golgotha is both history and mysterious super-history.

In no other form of execution is the human skeleton so em-phasized as in crucifixion. The basic structure of the human form is revealed on the cross, agonizingly extended. The sufferer on the cross has this basic structure thrust painfully into his con-sciousness, "he can count all his bones". Once again the Psalm connects "bones" and "death".

> A pack of hounds has surrounded me;
> The adversaries hedge me in.
> They have pierced my hands and feet.
> I can count all my bones.
> They gaze upon me with triumphant scorn.
> They divide my raiment among them
> And cast lots for my garment.

While the victim on the cross hears again the triumphant jeers of His enemies, he must even witness how they divide His rai-ment among themselves. A sensation of being finished and done with: the warm protective covering which has almost been part of His own being passes through strange and hostile hands. The "liquidation" of the human Being is anticipated in the Psalm in a nightmarish vision. The subtle veils of Man, woven of life and soul—these are the objects of lust of the Evil One. Thus the third wave of suffering, unmitigated by any comfort, has reached its climax. From this ultimate anguish of death the bitter cry for help rings out:

> *But Thou, Lord, be not far from me.*
> *O my strength, make haste to help me.*
> *Deliver my soul from the sword,*
> *My Ego-bearing soul from the hound of hell.*
> *Rescue me from the mouth of the lion*
> *And save me from the horn of the unicorn.*

The "Sword" too is a significant picture. In death the soul is severed from the body; the disembodied soul too has to face further painful separations. On earth the soul bore a varied mixture of higher and lower elements. After death it must painfully discard all that which cannot live in a higher world. The word translated "Ego-bearing Soul" is in the Hebrew *jechidah*, meaning "the One and only" (in the A.V. "Darling"). This phrase is used in the Kabbalah as the technical term for the highest faculty of the soul of man in which the spiritual Ego rules supreme and which gives him the unity and harmonious integration of his personality. This innermost centre is threatened by the powers of the underworld which appear again in the image of the hound of Hell. At long last the desperate cry from one threatened by death changes suddenly into the triumphant shout of the Redeemed.

IV

> *I will proclaim Thy name to my brethren,*
> *In the midst of the congregation I will sing Thy praise.*

We are not told in what form the rescue came. The words of the Psalm place only a hyphen, as it were, between the agony of death and the rescue. Only at the end of the Psalm do we find a hint of what is passed over here in silence. For the Psalm ends with the words "For He has done the Deed" (A.V. "That He hath done this"). Read in the light of the fulfilment in Christ, the hyphen implies the Deed of Easter.

This third time, when the wave of pain has grown into the agony of Death, neither the hymns of the fathers nor the recollection of childhood can bring comfort. Only a new, unheard of, Divine deed can counteract the doom of death. What we now know as the Death and Resurrection of the Son of God is hidden in the twilight of this prophetic Psalm in oracular words: For He has done the Deed (in the original, only "ki asah"—"for He did").

In the enthusiastic description of his redemption the Psalmist assumes more and more the role of the Prophet. Just as Christ asked Mary Magdalene to proclaim the Resurrection to His brethren, so the 22nd Psalm offers the message of joy to all humanity. The "great assembly" is like a prophecy of the Christian Church. While in the beginning the Psalm spoke of the "fathers", now it speaks of the "brethren".

> *All who fear the Lord, praise Him.*
> *Honour to Him from the sons of Jacob.*
> *Glory to Him from the seed of Israel.*
> *He has not despised the poverty of the poor.*
> *Nor hid His face from him.*
> *But when he cried to Him, He heard.*
> *My praise shall rise in the great assembly.*

God has adopted Man and his earthly poverty. In his joy and gratitude the Psalmist promises to fulfil a vow. He invites everyone to the great sacrificial meal which, like a Communion, follows the thank-offering in the Temple. In this picture, taken from Old Testament ritual, the sacred meal of Christ is foreshadowed, which will eventually communicate the Deed of Redemption to all human beings. The eucharistic spirit is beautifully expressed in the wonderful sentence, "Your heart shall live for ever".

> *I will pay my vows to the Lord in the sight of His worshippers.*
> *The poor shall eat and have their fill.*
> *All who look for the Lord shall praise Him.*
> *Your heart shall live for ever.*

The dynamic Redemption extends further and further. The pious Hebrew of old breaks through the limitations of his Jewish nation and reaches out to universal humanity. His poetic sentences sound like a promise of Whitsun.

The whole of humanity includes also those who have died. Eventually the vision reaches out even to them, and beyond them to the unborn souls, the coming generations.

The Psalm began with the cry "Why hast Thou forsaken me?" Over the second part, which praises the Redemption, this unspoken motto is written: "How hast Thou glorified me!"

The ends of the earth shall remember and return to the Lord,
All the kindreds of the nations shall worship before His countenance.
For the Kingdom is the Lord's,
He rules among the nations.
Him shall they worship that are laid to rest in the earth,
All those who have descended to dust bow low before Him.
For Him my soul shall live.
The future shall serve Him.
The Lord shall be proclaimed to the coming generations
And His righteousness to those who are yet to be born.
FOR HE HAS DONE THE DEED.

The Way of Life

PSALM 16

The 16th Psalm plays a special part in the history of Christianity. Together with two other quotations from the Old Testament it is quoted in Peter's address at Pentecost, the very first Christian sermon. The pouring out of the Holy Spirit released, for the first time, the power to proclaim publicly the historic deeds of Christ, the Mystery of Golgotha.

In this very first Christian message Peter refers to three passages from the Old Testament, corresponding to the three distinct parts of his address which are marked by the manner in which he addresses his hearers, and which expand step by step to universal humanity. "Ye men of Judaea and all ye that dwell at Jerusalem" —"Ye men of Israel"—"Men and brethren" (Acts 2; 14, 22, 29). In the first part (2; 14-21), Peter presents the outpouring of the Spirit as the fulfilment of the prophecy of Joel. In this context he speaks to begin with only of the spirit and its effects. But in the last verse of the first part, the call upon the Kyrios, the Lord, represents the passing over to the second part (2; 22-28), in which the world of the "Son" is described, the incarnation of Christ in Jesus of Nazareth, His Death and Resurrection. The third part (2; 29-36), proceeds from the Resurrection to the Sitting at the Right Hand of the Father. Here the Melchizedek Psalm 110 ("The Lord said unto my Lord: sit thou at my right hand") is quoted by Peter as a support for the understanding of his message. This third part leads into the sphere of God the Father sitting on His throne of majesty. It is significant that this very first Christian sermon should imply the Mystery of the Trinity.

The second part, then, which proclaims the fundamental Mystery of Death and Resurrection, i.e. the Mystery of the Son, is supported by Psalm 16. Peter wants to communicate to his hearer the incredible fact of his message and in order to help their understanding he quotes Psalm 16: "For David speaketh concerning Him . . ." (2; 25).

According to St. Luke who is the author of Acts, the risen Christ Himself revealed to His disciples the truth of the sacred Scriptures in His teaching during the forty days after Easter (Luke 24; 44). Apart from Moses and the Prophets, Luke specifically mentions the Psalms in this context. We may assume that after these instructions the time-honoured sacred texts appeared to the disciples in a new light and that these teachings of the Risen Christ inspired also Peter's Pentecostal address. We are justified therefore in regarding the original Hebrew text as potentially capable of development, open for future content beyond that of which its inspired author may have been conscious.

> *Preserve me, O God; I put my trust in Thee.*
> *I said to Yahwe: Thou art my Lord,*
> *I know of no good apart from Thee.*

This introduction is delicately coloured by the Mystery of the Trinity. To start with, a reference to being preserved, to putting one's trust—an experience of the Father. The Psalm speaks of the preservation of the human existence which is threatened from all sides and left in cold isolation. It is the Ground of the World from which all preservation, all maintainance of Being, proceeds.

But the Psalm does not stop there. It is not content with the preservation in the Father. The Psalmist knows that man is not meant to be only "child", but also to be "son". Thus he approaches God with a free act of loyalty. While the seeking for refuge was prompted by a kind of instinct of a higher order, the conscious relationship to God of the adult human being expresses itself in a definite "Word". "I said to Yahwe: Thou art my Lord". Man as spiritual personality confronts God face to face and decides for Him—a Son experience. This saying is a deed proceeding from the centre of one's being, a free vow. "Thou art my Lord", i.e. "Thou shalt give direction to my being."

The third sentence, "I know of no good apart from Thee", has again a different character. It implies a mental act which goes beyond a standing face to face. Man's consciousness surveys the whole range of values and expresses a judgment. It says ,"I know of no good apart from Thee". The "value" of God Whom the Psalmist considers as his higher self, as Lord, is measured in comparison with other "goods", and the result is: the Kyrios, the bearer of the higher Self, is not only the highest Good, "summum bonum", but "the" Good, the Good *kat' exochen*. All other "goods" deserve their name only inasmuch as they are related to this Kyrios. In these three steps: seeking refuge, free dedication, conscious judgment or values, we may discern the path from the Father to the Son and to the Spirit.

> *He finds His glory in the saints of the earth,*
> *His delight rests in them.*

This is how the somewhat uncertain words of the original text may have to be read. "He is glorified in the Saints." We hear a faint echo of the high priestly prayer in John 17, "I am glorified in them". The early Christians adopted the name of "Saints" although they were conscious of their human imperfections. They expressed thereby the conviction that they were touched and worked through by Powers of Salvation.

"His delight rests on them." Again we are reminded of a great fulfilment of this saying in the New Testament, "My beloved Son, in Whom I am well pleased", "In Whom I find the true reflection of my own being", "In Whom I am truly revealed".

But in contrast to the human beings who walk the way of salvation and sanctification there is also a negative choice.

> *They lay up fresh store of sorrows,*
> *Those that follow the other One.*

These are the people who do not open themselves to their higher beings, but surrender themselves to demonic powers.

In these demonic powers the Adversary is active, "the other One".

Their blood offerings I will not offer.

The worship of heathen Gods was a reality. St. Paul writes to the Corinthians, "Ye cannot drink the Cup of the Lord and the cup of Devils" (1 Cor; 10, 21). In the decadent cults of antiquity a definite relationship with the demons was achieved. The early Christian martyrs were rightly convinced that in making the required sacrifices they would feed the Demons. For this reason they refused inexorably to do so. However, the words of the Psalm are not out of date and perhaps only interesting from the historic view because those ancient sacrifices no longer exist; Devils and Demons are a reality even today. We can feed them without special ceremony and drink from their cup. Each evil impulse of soul feeds evil spirits and makes them stronger. They settle in like flies on dirt. Our blood, which registers the finest movements of our soul, is in reality the "special juice" at which the devil aims. Anyone who is inwardly open to evil concedes control over his blood to those powers who oppose God. Whether he know it or not, he makes a blood sacrifice.

I will not take their names on my lips.

This is still a valid truth today, although those rituals no longer exist in which the names of Demonic beings are recited in magic rituals. Evil words summon bad spirits. Swearing is in full reality a negative ritual. Not to recognize this fact is an unpardonable foolishness for men of the twentieth century. The Psalm now takes a positive turn.

The Lord is my lot and my cup.

In Psalm 116; 13 it is said "I will take the cup of salvation and call upon the name of the Lord". This verse has been incorporated in the liturgy of the Mass. It is the opposite to the sacrifice of blood and the invocation in the service of the demons.

The picture referring to "lots" is derived from the distribution of land. This distribution of land is in itself a parable. The religious man desires to settle and make himself at home in that spiritual region where God sustains and shelters his Ego. Then he is content with his "lot", even if he feels that he does not get a fair share of earthly goods. Now, after the reference to the cup, the Psalmist passes from the descriptive language of the third person to the direct address of the second person.

> *Yea, thou shalt be my inheritance for ever.*
> *No fairer lot could I win; my inheritance is full of delight.*
> *I will praise the Lord Who gives me counsel.*
> *My inmost life prompts me to do so in the seasons of the night.*

God has "given him counsel", has shared his inspiration with him. At night his inmost life responds with gratitude and praise. The A.V. says "reins" for inward life, literally "kidneys". The Old Testament frequently refers to the kidneys as the seat of the emotions. The organs hidden in the interior of the body were generally regarded as the vehicles of the inward life of the soul. In the New Testament, too, the Greek word *splangchna*, literally "bowels" (in popular language, "innards") signify the inwardness of soul. From this inwardness the voice of conscience is heard during the night and awakens a feeling of gratitude towards the Lord of Destiny.

Now we have reached the point where the quotation occurs which Peter uses in his Pentecostal address:

> *I have the Lord always before my eyes.*
> *He is at my right hand, I shall not be shaken.*

Hitherto the Psalm has spoken of turning towards God. Now it proceeds to a constant walking in the sight of God. The A.V. says, "I have set the Lord always before me: because he is at my right hand I shall not be moved". The expression "having set the Lord always before my eyes" refers more to the conscious mental relationship to God; the other picture of "having God at one's right hand" refers more to the Communion with God in one's will. The sense of the continued divine Presence protects us against being moved or upset or shaken. In other words, it guarantees the solid coherence of the personality. From this deepened link with God a totally new experience of life arises.

> *Therefore my heart is glad.*
> *My light-soul rejoices.*
> *My flesh, too, will dwell in trust.*

The three steps contained in this verse turn the experience inside out. It begins with the heart as the centre, and reaches outwards as far as the flesh, the physical body. Between the two, the mysterious word occurs which is translated "my glory" in the A.V. It is the Hebrew *kābôd* which is also used in the eighth Psalm as the Hebrew counterpart for *gloria* and *doxa*. The A.V. says "My glory rejoiceth". What can this mean?

In the Greek text of the address of Peter in Acts, the version of the Septuagint, the Greek translation of the Old Testament is followed. It by-passes the difficulty simply by replacing "kābôd" with "tongue": "My tongue was glad". Obviously the Hebrew word was no longer understood in this context even at the time of the pre-Christian translation of the Old Testament made in Alexandria. Modern translators sometimes render the phrase as "soul" because they assume that some such phrase must be intended.

A comparison with similar passages may be helpful. In Psalm 57; 8 and 108; 1 and 2 it says, "Awake up, my glory; awake, Psaltery and Harp."

"*Kābôd*" is *Gloria* and is normally used to express the revealing radiance or radiant revelation of God. But Man too has a radiance, which surrounds him as a subtle suprasensory part of his being. Man is not always conscious of this light which radiates from him. In his pedestrian everyday consciousness he knows nothing of his subtle etheric and astral veils. It is through music that his consciousness can be awakened to these subtle organisms. Thus the awakening of Psaltery and Harp is at the same time the awakening of the consciousness of Glory. It is not unlikely that the phrase which follows in Psalm 57; 8 and Psalm 108; 2, "I myself will awake early" points to a mystical experience. The

5

early dawn (aurora), has always been in the language of mysticism the picture of an inward process, from the Rishis of the Indian Vedanta who "awakened the dawn with potent spells" to Jacob Boehme's "Morgenröte im Aufgang".

A further instructive passage is Genesis 49; 6. The dying Patriarch Jacob blesses his sons. Looking at Simeon and Levi whose evil deed at Sichem he blames, he says "O my soul, come not thou into their secret; unto their assembly, mine honour, be not thou united". This is said at the moment of death. Jacob can no longer think of the physical appearance in the assembly of his sons. He considers the time which will follow after his death in which he will no longer be present in the body among his sons but will continue to influence them spiritually. When they hold council, when they assemble in solemn manner as the sons of their father, then, according to the wisdom of ancient days, the dead can be among them, not in their physical body, but in an etheric form of soul existence, in the subtle light-organism of "honour", of *gloria* or *kābôd*.

In our Psalm 16 *gloria* is placed between "heart" and "flesh", i.e. between the centre of the personality and the physical body. It can then only refer to a suprasensory reality which was no longer accessible to the consciousness of later times. It is in the heart of man that the divine joy arises. "Your heart shall rejoice", says Christ in His farewell discourses.

From this centre the divine joy passes over into the subtle etheric and astral organism of *gloria*—"My Glory rejoices"—and from there into the physical body. That which has its beginning in the inwardness of man eventually lays hold also of the external being of man. The ways of God end in the body. "My flesh too will dwell in trust". If the impressions of the communion with God are strong and lasting, eventually not only the subtle suprasensory organism, but even the physical body is affected. Other Psalms too speak of such comprehensive impressions of God. 63; 12: "My soul thirsteth for thee, my flesh longeth for thee in a dry and thirsty land". 84; 2: "My soul longeth, yea, even fainteth for the courts of the Lord; my heart and my flesh crieth out for the living God". Also the body shall be included in the redemption and transformation. *"Even my flesh will dwell in trust"*, does not only suggest that the religious man does not worry about his physical well-being. It is much more an anticipation of the Resurrection of the body, an expectation of that sensation which the early Christians possessed when they regarded communion as "the medicine of immortality".

Once again the Psalm now uses the form of addressing God in person.

> *For Thou wilt not leave my soul in Hades,*
> *Or allow Thy faithful servant to see corruption.*

Hades, in Hebrew *sheol*, in Greek *a-ides*, is the not-seeing, the darkness of the soul. In the days of old, people still preserved the knowledge that death is not the end of everything; but they expected nothing but a dull and shadowy existence; a second-rate existence in an Underworld which truly deserves its name. The souls had lost their native heavenly glory, "their divine nature", and found themselves after death in an emaciated existence of dark shadows. A dramatic description of this is contained in the eleventh book of the Odyssey, the Nekyia. These are not empty fantasies. Life after death lost its light in the measure in which souls became absorbed in earthly existence and grew into self-centred personalities. Only Christ's descent into Hell, His appearance among the dead, created a change. The Creed of the Christian Community says, "In death He became the helper of the souls of the dead who had lost their divine nature".

Once more we refer to Psalm 49. The souls appear like a "herd" which has no will, "death is their shepherd". "Like sheep they are laid in the grave; death shall feed on them."—"But God will redeem my soul from the power of sheol" (49; 14–16).

Holy Saturday carried new light into the realm of the dead. The promise is fulfilled "Thou wilt not leave my soul in the realm of the Shades". On Easter Sunday the Resurrection extends from the realm of the soul into the sphere of the body. The last enemy to be conquered is death. The reference to sheol is followed by the sentence, "Thou wilt not suffer thy faithful servant to see corruption". Peter quotes this saying as having been fulfilled through the Resurrection of Christ. David said it, "seeing before the Resurrection of Christ" (Acts 2; 31).

Although these are the decisive words, which matter to Peter, he begins his quotation from Psalm 16 earlier, when he says "For David speaketh concerning him, I foresaw the Lord always before my face". (Acts 2; 25.) Why should he first refer to these verses before he quotes the decisive sentence which speaks of the Resurrection? These sentences provide the basis for the promised Resurrection. The Resurrection is presented, not as an isolated, incomprehensible miracle, but as the final result of a gradual process, the fulfilment of a progressing evolution. It begins in the inmost centre with intimate decisions of the human heart. Then it proceeds to achieve an uninterrupted sense of the presence of God. The inward Easter radiates into the rhythm of the subtle organism, and reaches down at long last to the material body. Not only for purely external historic reasons is the Resurrection described at the end of the Gospels. The understanding of it can only be gained as the ripened fruit of an actual inward process of absorbing all the previous chapters, resulting in the conviction of Peter "Him God hath raised up having loosed the birth pangs of death (original Greek)—as it was really impossible that death should hold him" (Acts 2; 24).

Peter continues his quotation. He adds the phrase "Path of Life" and speaks of the joy in the sight of God. Way, path are old technical terms of the language of the mysteries describing the process of development which leads to initiation. It is significant that right at the beginning of the whole collection of Psalms the first Psalm presents immediately the picture of both paths—the path to death and the path to life. Similarly, also the Sermon on the Mount speaks towards the end of the broad way that leads to destruction and the narrow way which leads unto life. And Christ says Himself "I AM the way". He is Initiation personified. When Peter quotes the sentence of the way, he emphasizes once more that the Resurrection of Christ is the organic fulfilment of a path and that it can become accessible to us also when we follow this path ourselves.

> *Thou wilt show me the way of life,*
> *In Thy presence is fulness of joy,*
> *At Thy right hand loveliness for evermore.*

Thus the Psalm ends in the Hebrew original with a threefold harmony. The path which leads unto life, rightly understood, includes the Mystery of the Passion and of the Cross. The fulness of joy in the sight of God is an experience of Easter. "The right hand" refers to the Ascension. The fulness of grace (A.V. "pleasures") is a forestate of Pentecost. This last phrase means literally "loveliness". The right hand of God is not a blind tyrannical will to power, although it signifies also the idea of omnipotence, but a will to create, to create beauty, loveliness in the sense of the Latin *Gratia*, or the Greek *Charis*. Both words mean grace and gracefulness at the same time, graceful beauty. The Ascended Christ is, as our Creed says, "the Lord of the heavenly forces upon Earth, and lives the fulfiller of the Deeds of the Father, the Ground of the World." He mediates the creative activity of the right hand of God and, being the steward of the creative forces, he sends the Holy Spirit whose outpouring is celebrated at Pentecost. Pentecost, or Whitsun, a lovely festival, is celebrated at the time in which Nature shows its glorious array of colour in trees and flowers and all growing things, which are a visible parable of all that which the Spirit shall bring about on a higher level. The Old Testament does not only know the severity of the divine law. The 16th Psalm touches on the sphere of the Holy Spirit who graciously tends the flower gardens of a higher life. "At Thy right hand there is loveliness for evermore."

The last word is "evermore", eternity. The Psalm began with the prayer "preserve me". Now this preservation acquires its full and comprehensive meaning: to preserve the human being in its entirety and in the completeness of its constituent members from the threat of destruction.

The Creed of the Christian Community refers to those "who

are aware of the health-bringing power of the Christ", and it states that "they may hope for the overcoming of the sickness of sin, for the continuance of man's being, and for the preservation of their life, destined for eternity".

The Lord is my Shepherd

PSALM 23

I

The Psalm of the Good Shepherd is one of the best known. Its position in the Psalter is significant. The whole Psalter reflects the manifold shades of religious feeling in all the rainbow colours of the life of the soul. But this is especially true of the trio, Psalms 22, 23 and 24. The 22nd Psalm, "My God, my God, why hast Thou forsaken me?" is the Psalm of the suffering Messiah. It belongs to the dark side of the rainbow. The darkness of desolation grows into the blue of hope, and finally into the priestly purple of the act of sacrifice. The bright side of the rainbow shines in Psalm 24, in red and gold, the colours of Resurrection and Ascension. The Lord of Hosts, the King of Glory, is to make His entry. The Psalm of the Shepherd lies between the darkness of Psalm 22 and the brightness of Psalm 24. Calm and blessing, peace and healing stream from it, as from the green in the centre of the rainbow.

In its brevity, the 23rd Psalm is a perfect work of art. Its short concise sentences are all-embracing, something formulated for all time.

It belongs to the passages where the Old Testament approaches nearest to the sphere of Christ. In changed form it reappears in the tenth chapter of St. John's Gospel. "I am the Good Shepherd." We do the text no violence if we understand it in a Christian spirit. In doing so we put it in its proper light, as in fact so much in the Old Testament can only disclose its true depth and beauty in the light of the revelation of Christ.

The Lord is my Shepherd.
I shall lack nothing.

A "Shepherd" is one who bears in himself the spirit of a community. The great leaders of mankind were called in ancient times "Shepherds", because they did not egotistically shut themselves up in a private life of their own ("Shall I be my brother's keeper?"), but let the destiny of others live in their hearts. One who met such a "Shepherd" felt: I am not coming to someone who is a stranger, but to myself. What is best and most individual in me is at home in him.

The devout man of the Old Testament recognized his shepherd, the guardian of his eternal interests, in the God of the I AM. For this reason, Professor Hermann Beckh has translated the first verse of the Psalm: "He who speaks the I in me is my Shepherd". This God, the true "God of Man", appears in Christ. "I AM the Good Shepherd—I shall lack nothing." In all "lacking" the one great lack should be brought to our consciousness, the one from which our soul has suffered since the Fall, when it separated from the infinitely rich life of God. Speaking of the Good Shepherd Christ says: "I am come that they may have life and have it more abundantly". (John 10; 10.) The rest of the Psalm now describes the work of the Good Shepherd in a classical series of pictures.

He leadeth me to green pastures.

The soul has descended into earthly life in order to gain something there. When man moves about on earth so that his earthly life provides nourishment for his eternal nature, when he "gets something from it", then—speaking in the primitive and significant picture-language of old—the earth becomes a "pasture" for him. The Christ too in the chapter on the Shepherd speaks of "finding pasture" (John 10; 9). He leads us to the true "abundance" of our earthly existence, where the earth offers something, where we are not famished in our deeper being. The "green pastures" may also remind us of the green grass where Christ made the people sit down beside the lake for the Feeding of the Multitude.

If, however, the good Powers do not guide our earthly way, the earth becomes for our eternal self a grey wilderness, a dead and stony desert. Then we are "like a beast, led round in a circle on a barren heath by an evil spirit, while round about lies beautiful green pasture". (Goethe.) These words really apply to all those who only find a materialistic relationship to the earth. That is indeed the paradox, that the materialist in a deeper sense "gets nothing" from matter, since it is for him devoid of spirit. He may live in magnificent luxury, yet his soul remains desolate and poor. When he dies he has to leave all his riches behind, and over there he is truly a "poor soul". One who finds the spirit in terrestrial things takes his earthly experiences as a veritable possession with him over into the realm of eternity.

II

He leadeth me to fresh water.

We in our temperate climate scarcely guess with what elemental force the sunbaked Orient feels the divine in water. Of course, on a hot summer day after wandering long in burning heat and dust we are also more open to the magic sound of the words "water of life"; or when we water thirsty flowers.

In the original text the "fresh" water is water of "rests" (plural) *menuchôth*. It refers to moments of re-creation when what has been exhausted is built up again in the movement and streaming of etheric forces.

III

He restoreth my soul.

We know that our soul feels transformed near someone whom we revere, in whose presence we experience a kind of "well-being". So the nearness of the divine Shepherd is felt through an
5*

inner quickening. The soul is no longer a burden to itself, as happens when there is disharmony. The paralysing mood of depression disappears, and we regain our buoyancy and interest in life.

IV

He leadeth me in the paths of righteousness for his name's sake.

God's name is I AM. In the name of man God's name is to appear, in the I of man the I of God is to be manifest. The "I" name has been misused and dishonoured by man, the use of "I" has come to express egotism, selfishness. Therefore we pray: "Hallowed be Thy name". Our goal is to bring to light in our self our true eternal being, and not some egotistic caricature. We are only on the way to this. We must go through our destiny for the sake of growing our true I, for the sake of the eternal name. "He leadeth me in the paths of righteousness—for his name's sake."

Our true eternal name by which God called us into existence has not yet been realized; it hovers over our earthly form. It is written in the heavens, it may be read in the stars, but not as yet upon our brow. The star-names of all men dwell simultaneously in the name of Christ. We find ourselves when we find Him, the "Shepherd". He leads us along the path of destiny in the light of eternal righteousness for his name's sake and thereby also ours. When the goal is reached he will write our star-name on our brow.

V

But our path of destiny "for his name's sake" leads through the dark spheres of the adversary. Also when we are being led by the good Shepherd; yes, precisely then. No soul is spared the vale of darkness.

And though I walk through the dark valley, I
fear not evil; for thou art with me. Thy rod and
thy staff they comfort me.

The dark valley is a perfect picture for the material world, which prevents a free outlook and can become a nightmare. The soul whose home is in the bright realms of heaven must enter the narrow world of earthly time and space. It is gripped in a kind of claustrophobia. The child of light shivers in the sunless hollow, in the dark gorge. The cold breath of death reaches it, the hand of evil stretches out to seize it.

How many people have said these words about the dark valley in their prayers. Centuries, millenia have poured their fears and anxieties into them.

Notice the subtle change shown in the text. From the third person ("he leadeth me") we pass over to the direct "thou" of the second person. While it read just now, "He leadeth me upon the right way", it reads now, "for thou art with me". The reverent "He" now becomes direct address, speaking "face to face". Only when we enter into this still more inward relation to the divine Shepherd, can we overcome our anxieties and dangers. Only thus can we become fearless in the face of evil. The divine Shepherd takes charge of our higher Self.

Now the "thou" remains throughout the following verses. At the same time the Psalm finally abandons the pictures of Shepherd and beast and passes on to another series of images which are taken purely from human existence. The last picture relating to the Shepherd is the staff. "Thy rod and thy staff, they comfort me." But just as the shepherd-staff of Moses became after his call the powerful Staff of God, the kingly sceptre, so here too in the Psalm we may see in "the comforting staff" more than the ordinary shepherd's crook. The outstretched arm is a gesture of command. If the hand grasps the staff the authoritative gesture becomes still more expressive. The staff of Moses awoke the fountain of life from the rock. Pictures in the Catacombs show Christ performing the same miracle on Lazarus:

his staff touches the chamber of death, and Lazarus comes forth to new life.

VI

Thou preparest a table before me in the pres-
sence of mine enemies. Thou anointest my
head with oil, my cup runneth over.

After the awakening of Lazarus, he took part in the solemn repast in Bethany: "Lazarus was one of them that sat at table with him". (John 12; 2.) Whoever has found the "good Shepherd" as the higher Being whose Presence overcomes evil, is summoned to the feast of the Grail. "He sits at the Lord's table." But the Grail Castle is unthinkable without the opposing power of Klingsor. The Feeding of the Multitude by the lake occurs against the background of the death of John the Baptist, whose head lies on the charger. Judas into whom Satan has entered, leaves the room of the Last Supper and goes out into the night. Thus also in the Psalm the holy food is prepared "in the presence of mine enemies". One cannot come to Christ without having also looked the adversary and his hosts in the face. Without the conscious coming to grips with evil no higher development is possible. The writer of the 23rd Psalm may quite well have only thought of his ordinary enemies. There is no need to set aside this obvious meaning. But our ordinary enemies are only the representatives of much more dangerous powers who can kill more than the body. We perceive the mystical depths of this Psalm which realizes the fateful connection between the holy meal and the presence of the Adversary. St. John's Gospel says further of Lazarus who sat at the table of Christ in Bethany, that they sought to kill him. (12; 10.) The men who sought after his life represented the powers which would put to death the new seed of divine Life.

"Thou anointest my head with oil". One who partakes of the

holy meal goes through a consecration, is anointed as priest and king. His head is made to serve the Divine. *Christos*, the Greek translation of the Hebrew *Messias*, means in fact "the anointed one".

"My cup runneth over."—"I am come that they may have life more abundantly."

> *Goodness and mercy shall follow me all the days of my life and I will dwell in the house of the Lord for ever.*

"Goodness" is the innermost force of existence itself. In "mercy" this inner substance radiates outwards like the sun. Each human being has an invisible following which goes with him for evil or for good. The Book of Revelation says of the redeemed, "For their works do follow them".

Thoughts of eternity move through the soul of the Psalmist. A presentiment of Easter shines through his words: "I will dwell in the house of the Lord for ever". The Christian looks towards the Resurrection body that he is to receive, in which he will abide, dwell, survive, as in the true temple, in the house of the Lord. Man who is still a slave to the powers of sin must take leave of his body again and again in death. "The servant abideth not in the house for ever" (John 8; 35). Not until he is delivered through Christ from the sickness of sin can he dwell continuously in the Resurrection body.

No doubt the Psalmist means no more than a wish that it be granted him to dwell in the Temple of Jahve "to the end of his days". We find a similar wish expressed in the 27th Psalm: "One thing have I desired of Jahve, that will I seek after, that I may dwell in the house of Jahve all the days of my life, to behold the gracious beauty of Jahve and to meditate in his temple." (Compare also the 84th Psalm dealt with earlier.)

The Temple was the expression of the fact that God builds a "house"; it was a prophecy of the future dwelling of God in an earthly body. "But he spake of the temple of his body" (John

2; 21). The desire to be able to dwell in the house of God for ever was, in veiled form, the wish rising from the depths of the human being to dwell in the Resurrection body, for which the "house of God" is the prototype.

The Hymn of the Soul

PSALM 103

I

Praise the Lord, O my soul,
And all that is within me praise his holy name.

It is more than a figure of speech when Homer begins his Iliad by calling upon the Muse, "Sing to me, O Muse . . ." The Muse at that time was really an inspiring spiritual being, and Homer, who was a contemporary of David, was conscious of her co-operation. Equally, the German poet Klopstock begins his *Messiah* with the words, "Sing, immortal soul, of the redemption of sinful mankind". Homer summons the Muse that is still external to him. The Christian poet can call on the depths of his own soul.

Although Psalm 103 belongs to the ancient world, it anticipates the spiritual stream which leads to Christ in the human soul. So here, too, the Psalmist's own soul is to sound the praise of the Lord. The whole inner being, "all that is within me", with all its powers and possibilities shall echo the Holy Name. The holy "Name" is God in so far as He is known, in so far as He manifests Himself. The recognition of God and acknowledgment of His holy name in prayer, and the Hymn that this calls forth, demand the full compass of the soul's powers.

The spirit recognizes the Name of God, the soul attunes its feelings to this knowledge and merges with it fully. This feeling becomes inner music and then finally audible song. It becomes a Hymn of the soul moved by the experience of such precious

143

worth. The full significance of such related words as "praise", "prize" and "precious" has largely been lost through inflation: but the meaning common to them all is connected with the experience of worth.

> Praise the Lord, O my Soul, and forget not all
> his benefits.

People are much tempted to notice what is disagreeable, while the good they accept as a matter of course, without thought and hence also without thanks. Unless we cultivate gratitude consciously we make no progress on the path to God.

In the following lines the abundant benefits coming from God are stated one by one and placed gratefully before the conscious mind.

> Who forgiveth all thine iniquities;
> Who healeth all thine infirmities;
> Who redeemeth thy life from the grave;
> Who crowneth thee with grace and tender mercy.
> Who satisfieth thy longing with good things,
> And reneweth thy youth like the eagle.

The first three statements relate to a negative condition which is overcome through divine assistance, sin—sickness—death.

Sin working within is the root of all evil. The starting point for a comprehensive restoration of the whole threatened nature of man is to bring the soul into order. The result of sin is sickness. The sick soul encroaches on the region of the finer formative forces and makes them "sick". This is not meant to imply that every illness is therefore a direct result of sin. This would be a wrong conclusion which takes no account of the complex relationships of human destiny. That an individual suffers from a particular illness may arise from quite different factors in his life. But that disease in general is possible to mankind, that sickness and disease find access to man at all, is the result of sin.

The next step in the process by which sin becomes an integral part of the world, is death. This is why the sequence of the

Psalm is so organically right. It begins with the forgiving of sins, which brings the inner life into order. Then follows the healing of infirmities, just as Christ first forgave the palsied man his sins and afterwards made him whole. Finally, in the third place, comes the conquest of death. These are words which open up into future Christian times, having an enduring, even an increasing validity far beyond the life of the Psalmist. They are words which become increasingly right and true with the advance of Christian development.

The word *goel* in the original text has a special ring, "Who 'redeemeth' thee from the grave". The same word occurs in the significant passage in Job: "I know that my Redeemer liveth".

After sin, sickness, death have been disposed of, the positive side too is unfolded in a trinity of statements. The "crowning with grace and tender mercy" has a presupposition in what was called in the ancient Orient "the lifting of the head". The man who was broken down now rises up with his head into the higher worlds again, whose light shines down upon him in blessing.

After the crowning of the head, which restores the dignity of man, the Psalm turns to the heart. "Who satisfieth thy longing with good things." The deepest longing finds its fulfilment.

The working of grace in man penetrates lower and lower. "Who reneweth thy youth like the eagle." Ancient wisdom saw in the eagle the symbol for the transformation of the sinister powers of the scorpion. The "scorpion" which is active in the lower nature of man is a force which leads to death. When it is spiritualized, however, it turns into the "eagle". John the Evangelist has the eagle as his traditional symbol. He was the first to understand the resurrection of Christ. Surviving as "the centenarian of Ephesus" this disciple "whom Jesus loved" had known in himself the victory of renewal. "Behold, I make all things new." (Rev. 21; 5.) He had regained the forces of childhood on a higher level.

Isaiah also speaks of the "Eagle" with the same significance. "The youths become faint and weary and the young men fall. But they that wait upon the Lord acquire new strength, that they

mount up with wings as eagles, that they run and are not weary,
that they walk and not faint." (Isaiah 40; 30, 31.) The natural
forces of childhood and youth sooner or later fall into decline:
they must be found again in the spirit. Spiritual rebirth alone
rescues us from senile old age.

II

*The Lord executeth righteousness and judgment
For all that are oppressed.*

With these words the Psalm leaves the personal sphere of
individual salvation and praises the work of God on a grander
scale. The interpretation of the Old Testament has frequently
led to absurd difficulties, if it was all too narrowly assumed
that justice is to be found within one and the same span of life;
for as a rule the upright man is not at first rewarded with good
things and the evil man punished. The fundamental intuition of
God's justice is, however, not refuted by this. We must view
things from a wider angle by taking into account the possibility
of repeated lives on earth. Only in the great panorama of all our
earthly incarnations shall we be able to see how destinies are
controlled in justice by the highest Powers of heaven in their
fullness of love and wisdom.

It was this God, ruling with His justice the great course of the
world, who gave Moses insight into His ways.

*He made known his ways unto Moses,
His acts unto the sons of Israel.
The Lord is merciful and gracious,
Slow to anger and plenteous in mercy.*

Doubtless the unique hour is remembered which was granted
to Moses as the Lord passed before him, and proclaimed to him
his great Name in fullness. (Exod. 34; 5–7). The words, "Merciful and gracious is the Lord . . ." are a direct quotation from this
revelation to Moses.

He will not always reject us.
Neither will he keep his anger for all cycles of time.
He doth not deal with us after our sins,
Nor reward us according to our guilt.
For as the heaven is high above the earth,
So high is his mercy toward them that revere him.
As far as the sunset is from the sunrise
Doth he remove our transgressions from us.

"Wrath" is not the first state and will not be the last (cf. notes on Psalm 90). Even in pre-Christian times Moses knows God's willingness to forgive and to heal. Although He is a God of justice, a guarantor of the law of sowing and reaping, yet "he doth not deal with us after our sins". (cf. the chapter on Psalm 51.) If there were merely a rigid, automatic justice, striking back mechanically at the doer, man would be destroyed by the consequences of his deeds. He would "die in his sins". All the wrong that he had done to the world would simply annihilate him in its repercussion. But God adds something from His own substance. He gives a great, infinitely effective Divine Sacrifice as a new factor though which everything takes on a different appearance. Christ does not cancel the law of cause and effect, He does not overthrow the "karmic" law of destiny, but He graciously brings a quite new cause into the situation by binding Himself by a free deed of sacrifice to the destiny of mankind, so inserting Himself into the flow of Karma. The Law is not thereby set aside, for precisely by virtue of this law of cause and effect the Deed of Golgotha has its own far-reaching effect.

What is said of the righteous God who nevertheless does not allow us to be destroyed by the consequences of our deeds will only become fully comprehensible in the light of Christ. The God who does not reward man according to his iniquity is no capricious Sultan who arbitrarily seizes the reins of justice, but the God who is in the process of consummating the Christ-sacrifice for humanity.

And since this is so, one is not obliged to see the human being merely in his earthly aspect, as an imperfect man of earth—one would then have to give him up in despair of his future. But to the totality of the phenomenon "man" there belongs, too, the heaven of God that arches over him, full of promise of the future. It is no merit of man that this is so. The universe only tolerates him for the sake of his Christian possibilities in the future. He is only "justified through belief in Christ" because in process of becoming Christianized he will bring the world-scales of eternal justice into equilibrium again.

This in no way prejudices his freedom. The high heavens of grace which would fain be realized in earthly man are only for those who "reverently fear God". One condition must therefore be fulfilled on the part of man before grace can be put into operation. He must be conscious of his position, he must have reverent fear. In the New Testament this one condition means that he must believe in Christ, he must turn to Him. Otherwise the high heavens of grace above him cannot reveal themselves, and in the last resort he must "die in his sins". The factor of redemption cannot then be inserted into the account of his destiny.

"As far as the rising is from the setting." We belong through our sins to a world which is going down, which is "setting". Grace unites us with a new morning of the world. Through grace a different world rises in us, separated from the world of our sins by inconceivable distances.

We see man in great dimensions. Man, as he has the high heaven of grace over him, and as he belongs to a cosmic morning, while his sins go down into a cosmic evening.

The following sentence also has a New Testament ring:

> Like as a father pitieth his sons
> So the Lord pitieth them that reverently fear him.

The Godhead who sends the Redeemer sees our frailty.

> For he knoweth our frame;
> He remembereth that we are dust.
> As for man his days are as grass:

As a flower of the field so he flourisheth,
The wind passeth over it and it is gone;
And the place thereof shall know it no more.
But the grace of the Lord is from everlasting to ever-
lasting upon them that reverently fear him,
And his righteousness unto the sons of their sons,
To such as are true to his covenant
And to those that remember the aims of his will to
realize them.

The "dust of the earth", transitoriness, has entered into man. But the Old Testament also knows of the breath which God breathed into man, and it tells of a creation of man (Gen. 1; 27), long before the transitory, earthly form was allotted to him (Gen. 2; 7). Man, through his share in the eternal, is able to make a covenant with God. His fidelity to the supersensible raises him above the merely transitory. "Fidelity" assumes that there is a lasting element in us, it is a function of the ego.

III

The Psalm began with the Hymn of the Soul. It ends with a Hymn of the Universe. What began in the inmost circle is now carried out into the cosmos.

The Lord hath set up his throne in the heavens;
And his kingdom embraceth the universe.
Praise him, ye his angels,
Ye heroes of strength that do his word,
To carry the voice of his word to the world,
Praise him all his shining hosts,
Ye exalted servants that accomplish his will.

The heart's song of praise unites with the song of sacrifice of the hierarchies. The Act of Consecration of Man speaks of this at Christmas, giving the names of the nine angelic orders. The

divisions of the ranks of angels is lightly touched upon, somewhat as in Psalm 104. There are first the Angels, who as in the
Greek *angeloi* are simply called Messengers. They bring messages
from spirit to spirit. "Heroes of strength" probably indicates the
middle hierarchy. They live actively in the sphere of sound and
carry it powerfully into the world. The word "hosts" *sabaoth*
carries us to the highest Hierarchy. *Sabaoth* is occasionally used
for the "starry" hosts, for instance in Jeremiah 33; 22 as "hosts
of heaven" that cannot be numbered. To this highest hierarchy
belong the "exalted servants" (cf. remarks on Psalm 124), the
Liturgents, as they are called in Greek. They live in the immediate
substance of the divine will. The Psalm says: "they accomplish
his Will".

Then, finally, our gaze is turned to the whole of creation:

> *Praise him all his works,*
> *In all places of his dominion.*

The concluding sentence turns back once more to the beginning. But in the meantime the soul has widened out and made
the whole universe its concern. The soul's song of praise now
resounds with the Hymn of the Worlds.

> *Praise the Lord, O my Soul.*

The Future of the Earth

PSALM 37

I

The Psalm begins with the admonition not to waste the forces
of the soul in hatred of evil.

Be not inflamed against evil-doers nor be
over-zealous against the workers of iniquity.

How much energy of the soul is lost in this way. There is no
doubt a great temptation to be annoyed from morning to night
over one thing or another which is not what it ought to be. But
righteous anger firing our energy is only useful where we can
improve things. In the first place in self-discipline, dealing with
our own failings. Beyond this, being "inflamed" and "over-
zealous" soon becomes unfruitful. Important forces of our soul
—needed in a positive direction—are used up to no purpose.

We should leave what is evil to its own unreality. At any rate,
we do not share the view of some writers of the Old Testament,
where it is imagined that the doom of evil must become evident
in this life. We take broader views; although the early concept
remains right in principle—that evil has its own judge.

The energies of the soul should flow towards the Divine, not
waste themselves in fruitless anger.

Trust in the Lord and do good,
Inhabit the land and strive for faithfulness.

Into this expression "trust in the Lord" we may as Christians read all that our relation to Christ can be. This relationship of heartfelt confidence can also enable us to do good.

Psalm 37 circles continuously round the word *erez*, the earth, the land; to begin with, quite concretely the land of Israel, the Holy Land. Theological interpretation explains the Psalm as showing the pious, the *Chassidim* in contrast to the others who fell away from the Jahve religion and became subject to foreign influences. The conflict centred round the Holy Land, and which of the two parties should control it. The Psalm acquires its significance however from the fact that this particular conflict between two groups of men, long since relegated to the past, can be a symbol of a much greater problem. Behind the contest of the "pious", among whom perhaps many narrow-minded fanatics could have been found, and the so-called "godless" to control the land, there appears a much greater and more significant conflict: the fight of the good and evil powers for the leadership of the earth. The devout are then the men of the future who serve the Christ, and their adversaries are the powers of anti-Christ, and *erez* is then not only the land but the earth.

The actual theme of the Psalm is the apocalyptic contest for the earth. That will become clearer still in what follows.

"Inhabit the land and cultivate faithfulness." It was right for Abraham to depart from his fatherland and his friends. Whether a man travels to distant lands or remains at home his whole life long, differs for each individual according to his destiny. The Psalm does not intend to decide this question. It is concerned with who is to possess the land. This fight for the Holy Land depends ultimately on the inner qualities, the inner character of the people; it is more than a political question. It has apocalyptic significance, "Inhabit the land in the right way by keeping faith with the spirituality which thou servest".

This gives to the Psalm its lasting importance and actual quality. Then this sentence, freed from its temporal, historical limitation, reads, "Inhabit the earth in the right way". Acknowledge the fact that you are not an inhabitant of heaven to whom the earth is strange, but—although of heavenly origin—you have been placed upon the earth by the wise powers of destiny. Affirm this fact! Cultivate the right loyalty to the earth and thereby serve the spiritual worlds in obedience.

In the end this can be fully understood only in the spirit of Christ. For Christ Himself has chosen the earth. With the Resurrection He has created the seed of a transformed, spiritualized earth which is linked with heaven in a new way. "We are engaged in a mission: we are called upon to transform the earth." These words of Novalis are genuinely Christian. In the idea of transformation man keeps faith both with heaven and earth. He brings the two together so that the great apocalyptic marriage may come about. The Christian cannot simply wish "to get to Heaven", he must bring to heaven the earthly element, purified and transformed. He cannot merely wish to possess the earth, he must bring the spirit into it.

This is the theme of the 37th Psalm. It enjoins fidelity to the earth together with fidelity to the spirit.

II

We must not overlook the fact that the following verses, so very well known, come immediately after "Inhabit the land in true fidelity".

Find thy blessedness in the Lord.
He shall give thee the desires of thine heart.
Commit thy way unto the Lord
And trust in Him. He will bring it to pass.

We are here on the sacred ground of the mystic. We see that the Old Testament does not merely recognize obedience to the Law. It is also aware of the inner blessedness which is vouchsafed through communion with the divine presence.

The idea is widespread among Christians that religion has largely to do with praying to God for this or that. Many people only remember God when they need something, when they

want to have something, when they want to be relieved of some
affliction. The Psalm is on a very different level. The Psalmist
knows that the first thing in religion is worship, meditation, the
blessedness of gazing upon and experiencing the Divine in forgetfulness of self. Only one who returns to himself again from a
selfless adoration of the Divine, may now utter his petitions. The
Lord's Prayer begins by addressing "Our Father", which rightly
understood involves a contemplation of God. From this meditation the three petitions proceed which are not yet related to man's
earthly needs, but are characterized by "thy"—"thy name", "thy
kingdom", "thy will". Only then, cleansed and purified by what
has gone before, may we come to our earthly affairs, "our daily
bread".

And so the first sentence of the Psalm speaks of the blessedness
which we shall find in the Lord. Then follows the second, "He
shall give thee the desires of thine heart". It can then no longer
be a foolish request or egoistic desire to get something in which
we should like to interest God. True prayers, worthy of being
heard, come from selfless worship; only then are they really
desires of the "heart". That is indeed a different thing from what
one generally connects with the ordinary phrase "my heart's
desire". To the Christian prayer, fulfilment is promised when it
is uttered in the name of Christ. Of course, we need not always
end our prayers by the formula "for Christ's sake". "For Christ's
sake" means rather that we should first completely permeate
ourselves with His being. Out of this real uniting with Him "Ask
what ye will and it shall be done unto you", for then this "what
ye will" has taken on a different character: then it will truly be
desire of the pure heart.

A mystical experience like this is the source of the famous words
which now follow: "Commit thy way unto the Lord". It is the
way of destiny, to tread which you have been sent to earth by the
wisdom of the higher worlds. Surrender yourself with confidence
to divine guidance. The words "trust in him" (as in verse 3) are
once more repeated. "He will bring it to pass". He will do it.
This is no invitation to passivity. Such words must not be isolated.

THE FUTURE OF THE EARTH

They are preceded by "Trust in him". Do good. Inhabit the land
in true fidelity. Find thy delight and blessedness in the Divine.
This all points to activity on the part of man. For even "beatitude", which is the state of finding delight in the Spirit, is something that must be sought for. Only through the inner activity
of achieving quiet moments for prayer and reading can we attain
to true and healthy tranquillity. "Commit thy way unto the Lord.
He will bring it to pass. He will do it." We only set divine inter-
vention really in motion through our right surrender, just as in
the Communion Service of the Act of Consecration of Man the
"offertory" with our united devotion precedes the consecration
of the elements, when God "brings it to pass", and "does it".
(We have already met this mysterious saying that God will "do
it", in the final verse of Psalm 22, the Passion Psalm of the
Redeemer.)

> *And he shall bring forth thy righteousness as*
> *   the light,*
> *And thy judgment as the bright noonday.*

Christ says, "Then shall the righteous shine forth as the sun
in the kingdom of their Father". (Matt. 13; 43.) Nothing is lost
that was well and truly done, even though it may seem at first to
have no results. Nothing is really wasted. With all that we accomplish of real value we are building a future world. What is
now inward morality will one day become "nature". The right
deeds that have been done on earth will one day illumine a coming
world just as the sun shines upon us today. The fact that goodness
will one day be rehabilitated and honoured is the wider perspec-
tive of these words of the Psalm, beyond their more obvious
meaning. This will come about in its most sublime form when in
the future the inner light will shine forth from man and become
world-light; for Christ's words about the upright who shine like
the sun, and the destiny of his disciples to be the light of the
world ("Ye are the light of the world" Matt. 15; 4) cannot be
understood concretely enough.

> *Incline thy silence to the Lord and hope in Him.*

Be still to the Lord. Keep silent to Him. Again words that let one guess at a whole world of self-training and mystical blessing. We must grasp the dative case in these sentences. Keep silence to the Lord. This silence is not a brooding in oneself, it is an inner turning towards the divine. We bring all else in us to rest and hold the soul, emptied of all other content, like a chalice to the Divine, so that it may enter into this emptiness and fill it. We incline the cup of our soul to God that He may pour in His divine life—that is the meaning of this dative.

III

The Psalm has such wide horizons through the fact that it weaves together these two themes: the inner state of mystical blessing, and interest in the great events of the world.

> *Be not inflamed against him who prospers in his*
> *way although his acts are strangers to God.*
> *Cease from anger, forsake wrath,*
> *Be not inflamed; it only leads to evil.*
> *For the evil-doers go to their downfall.*
> *Those that wait upon the Lord*
> *They shall inherit the land.*

We are immediately reminded of one of the Beatitudes in the Sermon on the Mount; for Christ's mind lived in the Psalms. "Blessed are the meek for they shall inherit the earth." (Matt. 5; 5.) "The meek, i.e. those who by conquering their elementary passions have become master of themselves, have attained to the goal of the earth. The spirit-self is the silent power of conscience which transforms the raw material of the soul's instincts and in-clinations into calm and collected humanity." (E. Lenz.) Meek-ness is not inner slackness and weakness, but the inner conquest, the calming of the waves of passion. The meek are those who keep in check the soul-forces which want to dissipate themselves in fruitless heat and irritation, those who can actively restore silence in the soul. What is achieved inwardly produces an effect in the world itself. "They shall inherit the earth." The "earth" *ge* in the original Greek of the Beatitude is the very word *erez* in the Psalm. In the Beatitude it no longer has the limited meaning of "the land", it is the earth as a whole, the earth as a world. The inner conquests and achievements of man ultimately decide the destiny of the planet. Moreover the Beatitudes are immediately followed by the words: "Ye are the salt of the earth". The earth itself is at stake.

In the end the earth will not belong to those who have only made it an object of exploitation from which to derive their pleasures and desires. Such men "get" nothing from the earth in the true sense of the word. It is a basic experience that it is just the materialist who, in a deeper sense, possesses nothing of the earth. Only one who looks at the earth in a spiritual way can "inherit" it and really get something out of it. For instance, a man may own a park without having an eye for the beauty of the trees and the green of the lawns. Another, to whom this does not belong, can open himself to all this beauty and take it into his heart. Which of the two "inherits" the park, which gets something out of it as the real owner? He who has taken it into his inner being carries the terrestrial, spiritually transfigured, over into the other world and preserves it in his own immortality. The other only possessed it externally. When he dies he can carry nothing of it away, but must leave it behind. He has had nothing from his possession and "on the other side" he is a poor soul.

The earth as a material globe is turning to dust. But of its true being we must carry over something into eternity. Those who would snatch and grab for themselves obtain nothing from the earth that it could actually bestow on them; they lose the earth in possessing it.

The expression "inherit the earth" which was held worthy of inclusion in the Beatitudes is continually found as a recurring verse in the 37th Psalm, in manifold forms:

Those that look to the Lord in expectation shall inherit the earth (v. 9).

The meek shall inherit the earth (v. 11).
They that are blessed of him shall inherit the earth (v. 22).
The righteous shall inherit the earth (v. 29).

We can make these four different aspects somewhat more concrete if we look at the four parts of the Act of Consecration of Man* which follow each other according to the same inner law.

The first: "to look towards the Lord in eager anticipation"—that is the mood in which we listen to the Gospel.

The second: "the meek", literally "those who are bowed down"—these are they who are capable of sacrificial devotion to the divine.

The third: "those whom he has blessed"—the consecration is the great experience of blessing, which as divine love descends upon the earthly elements and transfigures them.

The fourth: "the righteous"—these are not the self-righteous who want to "do works before God" and count on God for their deserts, but those into whose own being the divine righteousness is poured out. One who receives the Communion in full reality becomes righteous thereby; he brings the great cosmic scales which were thrown out of balance by the Fall into equilibrium again.

The following sentence stands between the third and the fourth aspect:

> *Depart from evil and do good.*
> *Thou shalt dwell in eternity.* (v. 27.)

This "dwell" is something similar to the Johannine "abide". The theme of "earth" is concluded in the comprehensive sentence:

> *Fix thy attention upon the Lord and keep his way,*
> *He shall exalt thee to inherit the earth.* (v. 34.)

Keep his way, which through the humility of the Offering,

* The central Service of the Christian Community. Its four main parts are: Gospel, Offertory, Consecration, Communion.

the blessing of Consecration, and through the Communion of righteousness, leads you to the inheritance of earth, inwardly acquired.

The Beatitude of the Meek has a relationship with the Beatitude of the Peacemakers. There is a foretaste of this in verse 37 which may be literally translated as follows:

> *Preserve the right and cultivate uprightness;*
> *for a future belongs to the man of peace.*

Future, in Hebrew *acharith*, means "that which is after". Many commentators see in this sentence only the well-known ancient Jewish hope for descendants, for bodily fertility. But even if the Psalmist had only meant that "the devout man has posterity whereas the posterity of the wicked perishes" (v. 38), it points to a deeper meaning. It is true, past Ages experienced the future in children, but this experience went beyond the mere continuity of the family. The children of the body are a symbol for the fact that each human being is also inwardly endowed with a future. The seed of a future development stirs within him, which will come to light, will "de-scend", when the human form in which he now appears will have passed away. The New Testament calls this true human form of the future "the Son of Man", which since it has been created out of the Divine, may also be called "the Son of God". "The seed of God is within us." "It doth not yet appear what we shall be." (I John 3; 9 and 3; 2.)

It need not be a physical reality when the Psalm says that the posterity of the wicked will be exterminated. But the deeper truth holds good: evil is without a real future and is "humanly unfruitful". On the other hand, "A future hath the man of peace".

What promise does the Christ make to the peacemakers in his Beatitude? "For they shall be called Sons of God." The ancient world would have said, "For they will acquire sons". We hardly need to point out that in Christianity, too, it is a high and holy task of man to pass on life. In the New Testament the inner application is stressed: the man of peace is to become fruitful in himself, he must progress towards his true human form as bearer of the divine forces of the future. "For they shall be called Sons of God."

"A Fortress Strong . . ."

PSALM 46

Luther's famous hymn "A fortress strong is our God" was inspired by Psalm 46. If we consider this Psalm more closely, we observe that it reaches still more deeply into the apocalyptic sphere than the stirring hymn of the Reformation. For this reason it may have a significant message for us today.

I

The word "God" stands at the beginning of the Psalm not by chance. If we desire to find a fresh relationship to the sacred ancient text, we must contemplate and worship together with the inspired poet this supreme and ultimate reality. From there a bridge is built towards us and our need. "God is our refuge and our stronghold, a ready help in peril."

From such experience of God's gracious and ready help these words emerge, "Therefore we have no fear, even if the world perished and the mountains be carried into the midst of the sea". This sentence has frequently been compared with a line by Horace, "*Si fractus illabatur orbis, impavidum ferient ruinae—* though the whole world may break up, its ruins shall kill a fearless one". The stoic philosophy aspired to a sovereign control of the world based on the realization of man's spiritual dignity. But this control could only be maintained, if on the other hand the sensitivity for the world and its pressure was weakened. "Ataraxia" was the goal, the complete imperturbability, which regards catastrophes with cool detachment and is never "impressed".

In the Psalm the immediate and concrete experience of God is the basis for the intrepid soul. With this experience the religious man can afford to embrace with his feeling heart even the horrors of the world. His feelings will not remain unaffected by calamities. He will be affected by them in the way in which a natural unsophisticated heart would expect to be affected. With open eyes and open heart he can face them, because he knows his inward being supported and carried by the divine powers which are stronger than all destruction. Religious fearlessness does not arise from a contempt for all terror, but from the strength which is rooted in the eternal.

Thus the vision of the Psalmist can venture into the future in which apocalyptic catastrophes threaten to occur. His gaze points in the same direction as later that of St. John on Patmos. Like John he is confident that the divine help can always be found, and will lead the faithful through all peril and destruction.

It has been conjectured that the Psalm might have been written after the unexpected liberation of Jerusalem through the surprising retreat of Sanherib who had laid siege to the city. Whatever may have been the historic reason, the apocalyptic vision of future oppressions and liberations on a vast scale is what matters. The Psalm speaks of nothing less than the end of the world itself. "Even if the world were scattered and the mountains carried into the heart of the sea". The mountains with their age-old solidity and stability seem to guarantee to man the security of earthly existence; yet they are only relatively "everlasting". One day even they will no longer be. But when at such profound transformation even that vanishes which seemed to be lasting, the God-filled Ego of man should be by then so much consolidated that it can ride out all these storms.

The raging sea has always been a picture for the unbridled forces of swirling chaos. "The waters rage and roar, the mountains tremble before their unleashed fury." The Old Testament contains here and there remnants—like megalithic remains—of most ancient mythological conceptions of creation. Prophets and Psalms allude at times to a primeval battle which the Divine

Creator waged against the Serpent of Chaos, called Leviathan or Rahab, which appears as a sea monster. Creation is, in the last analysis, a wrestling of an organizing principle with the wild forces of sheer vitality. Untamed they cause chaos. But without this "raw-material" creation would remain anaemic.

The ancient mythologies seem to have known that the gigantic battle with the forces of chaos which occurred at the beginning of the world, will have to be fought again at the end. Comparative religion registers such facts, but refrains from asking: do they contain any truth, were these dreamers and poets perhaps true seers, do their pictures make sense?

Psalm 46 does not explicitly name Leviathan or Rahab, but "the raging and roaring waters" are clearly an apocalyptic vision. Once again the powers of the abyss will raise their head.

The Hebrew word "Selah", which may indicate a musical interlude but may also mean something like "proceed on a higher level" marks the end of the first section of the Psalm. It is repeated at the end of the 2nd and 3rd section.

> *God is our refuge and our stronghold*
> *A help found in peril, indeed.*
> *Therefore we have no fear,*
> *even if the world perished and changed throughout*
> *and the mountains be carried into the heart of the*
> *seas.*
> *The waters rage and roar.*
> *The mountains tremble before their unleashed fury.*
> Selah.

II

In the Book of Revelation the seer beholds the souls who are united with Christ gathered in the city of God, the heavenly Jerusalem, while the old world perishes. Christian humanity continues to live thereafter in a higher, changed form of existence, as it is revealed in the hieroglyphic picture of the "heavenly city".

The second part of this Psalm speaks in its own manner of this higher Jerusalem. A literal translation would say: "A river—its branches gladden the city of God". This is what it says: "A river—". A plain and clear vision. It is the picture of the divine River of Life.

In our normal consciousness we never see "life" itself, only living things. For higher vision, however, this mysterious fluid which we call "life" appears in the image of running water,* a mighty river. "And the angel showed me the river of life, clear as crystal", says St. John in his description of the heavenly Jerusalem. The river of paradise is restored. Now it flows through the holy city which is at the same time the world of God and the world of men. In the historic Jerusalem such a river never existed. Zachariah and Ezekiel saw the future city of God, when they saw this river rise in "Jerusalem". (Zach. 14; 8: Ezek. 47.) Of this river also the Psalm speaks.

Then the Psalmist observes how the river divides into many branches, and waters the whole city. In contrast to the floods of chaos this water of life is ruled and directed by the wisdom of God. In its many divisions it is, as it were, individualized. For this life which pulsates everywhere "delights" the city of God, it spreads joy and bliss everywhere.

It is "the city of God, the sanctuary of the dwelling of the highest God". The "highest" is "Eljon" in Hebrew. Such was called the God whose priest Melchizedek met Abraham in Jerusalem with bread and wine and blessed him in the name of "the highest God". Abraham encountered then a still higher manifestation of God than the One Whom he himself served. He Who revealed Himself through Melchizedek was related to Abraham's own experience of God as the sun to the moon. A ray of the future sun of Christ touched him. The God Who dwells in the city which is watered by the rivers of life, is none other than this "highest God" whose ritual is celebrated with

* Cf pages 27 and 56.

bread and wine. With the word "Eljon" the ancient sacred tradi-tion of Jerusalem is touched upon. "God dwells in her midst, she stands unmoved. At break of dawn he comes to her rescue."

Not before this second part, in connection with the heavenly Jerusalem, does God come really close to man. Only through their fulfilment in Christ do the images of the second section become fully transparent. Of the incarnate Son of God it is fully true that "he dwells in the midst of the city". And the resurrection which is an event of day-break, is the dawn of a new world. It is in truth the fulfilment of the sentence, "With break of dawn he comes to her rescue".

The powers of evil are incapable of touching this world of Christ which rises from the ruins of the perishing world. "Nations may be in turmoil, kingdoms totter. Before his voice the earth dissolves." The section concludes with this shout of joy: "the Lord of Hosts is with us, the God of Jacob is our fortress".— Yahweh Sabaoth is the Lord of the host of stars in which the angelic hierarchies were at home. "With us"—in Hebrew *émmanu*. This is reminiscent of the name which is given to the Saviour by Isaiah, *Emmanu-EL*, "with us God".

The "God of Jacob" is the God who puts man's strength and stamina to the test, who makes him wrestle with obstacles. He is the God to Whom Jacob said, "I will not let thee go, except thou bless me".

It is remarkable how in this second part of the Psalm the various names of God come together: God (Elohim), Lord (Yahweh), the Highest (Eljon). It belongs to the mysterious quality of Christ Who dwells within man, that the Divinity is revealed in fullness and called by different names.

> *A river!—Its branches spread delight*
> *through the city of God,*
> *the sanctuary of the dwelling of the Highest God.*
> *God dwells in her midst,*
> *She stands unmoved.*
> *With break of dawn he comes to her rescue.*

Nations may be in turmoil.
Empires totter.
His voice resounds,
The earth dissolves.
The Lord of Hosts is with us.
The God of Jacob is our fortress.

Selah.

III

If one considers the 3rd section from the point of view of history, one can read it as the description of the citizens of Jerusalem emerging through the gates of the City into the open to look over the battlefield after the besieging armies have withdrawn. "Come and see the marvellous deeds of the Lord, who does stupendous things on the earth." But again the spectacle of the broken and abandoned arms lying round about inspires a more far-reaching apocalyptic vision. The Psalm speaks of the God who "breaks the bow, shatters the spear, and burns the chariot in the fire". God's laws maintaining everlasting life will prevail. God hands destruction over to the destroyers: in the end war liquidates itself, destruction destroys itself. Destructive forces meet with their own destruction. Today in the atomic age we can form a realistic picture of war reducing itself *ad absurdum*.

The vision of destruction destroyed is followed immediately by a call to awaken a higher consciousness. The original Hebrew simply says: "Desist". It means quite concretely: "Desist from warfare". But we should not give up warfare simply for reasons of expediency or fear. The constructive action is to lift the soul to a higher consciousness. Man should recognize God who says I AM. He can only be recognized through the "I" in man. He will not be found in dim collective instincts, but in the very centre of the human personality which has come of age. He waits to be recognized and acknowledged freely and voluntarily by the individual human being while He sanctifies the individual "I" towards selflessness. He prepares it for a new and higher form of community. This God of the free "I" has come in Christ among men.

Apart from the ordinary word for "I" (*ani*) the Hebrew language possesses a solemn "grand form" for it: *Anokhi*. It is "I AM" written in capitals. This "I" writ large is used here. "Know this: that I AM God". With this element of "knowing" the third Person of the Holy Trinity, the Holy Spirit, is also touched upon.

The following verse reads in the Authorized Version, "I will be exalted among the heathen, I will be exalted in the earth". The divine I AM, which to begin with is hidden to man in the narrow, egocentric darkness of his soul, rises up in power. HE can no longer be overlooked and ignored. HE would fain become the decisive factor in the life of humanity on earth. The development and transformation of this saying is found in the New Testament, when Christ speaks of the Cross and says, "And I, if I be lifted up from the earth, will draw all men unto me". (John 12; 32.)

> *Come and see the marvellous deeds of the Lord*
> *Who does stupendous things on the earth.*
> *He maketh wars to cease*
> *Unto the end of the earth.*
> *He breaks the bow,*
> *He shatters the spear,*
> *He burns the chariot in the fire.*
> *Desist—and know that I AM God.*
> *I will be exalted among the heathen,*
> *I will be exalted in the earth.*
> *The Lord of the heavenly hosts is with us;*
> *The God of Jacob is our fortress.*
>
> Selah.

"Sit Thou at my Right Hand"

PSALM 110

The picture of Christ sitting at the right hand of the Father has always been connected for Christians with the event of the Ascension. Modern man cannot accept this picture, because he takes it in a spatial sense and so regards it as absurd. But the Ascension is not an outward process. It is a visionary experience of the Apostles, who perceive that Christ is raised to a higher order of being. He now shares in a non-finite heavenly form of being, in which He can for the first time really carry out His promise: "I am with you always". Now at last He can really be "with us" in His divine presence everywhere on earth. Similarly, Christ's "sitting at the right hand of the Father" is also a visionary picture, which should not be taken in a physical sense. Sometimes we say about a man who acts completely in accordance with the will of another, that he is his "right hand". Thus the ascended Christ is "the fulfiller of the deeds of the Father, the Ground of the World", as the Creed of the Christian Community expresses it.

What does this mean? Christ, the "Son", is first experienced by human beings as a power within them. But he is able ever more and more to radiate outwards from within, and can finally influence the whole being of a man, even his body and blood. Man's body and blood stem from very high Powers who are so strong that they can carry over spiritual being into physical being. They are "magic" forces, in the noblest and purest sense, which are able to bridge the gulf between spirit and matter; that is, they are primal, divine Father-forces. So when the Christ who has first been experienced in a purely inward way begins to extend His working right into the depths of the bodily organism, He is working together with the Father-forces. In that He is capable of transfiguring our body from within, and finally of wresting it from Death itself, He "sits at the right hand of the Father".

This descriptive phrase, which plays such an important part in the New Testament, is taken from the 110th Psalm. It is Christ Himself who quotes this Psalm, when He wishes to show the Pharisees that the Messiah must certainly be of a higher order than a mere descendant of David (Matt. 22; 44). In the New Testament the 110th Psalm is quoted most often. It is also exceptional in that it mentions by name the mysterious Priest-King Melchisedek, who comes into the story of Abraham but does not appear anywhere else in the Old Testament.

Christ's conversation with the Pharisees shows that the 110th Psalm was applied by the representatives of Judaism to the Messiah at that time. It was possible for Christ to presuppose the view that when David, the author of the Psalm, says, "the Lord (God) said to my Lord, 'sit thou at my right hand'," he meant by "my Lord", the Messiah. It was only later on, when opposition to Christianity played a part in Jewish religious life, that the Rabbis took up the very forced interpretation that the reference was to Abraham. And it is not without interest that it was a representative of Jewish esoteric teaching, the Cabbalist Obadia Sforno, who upheld the connection of the 110th Psalm with the Messiah.

*   *   *

The Psalm begins, in a particularly solemn mood, with a word which actually means "whisper", and suggests a secret, divine breathing in, or inspiration.

> *A Psalm of David. Whispering of the Lord*
>   *to him, who is my Lord:*
> *Sit thou at my right hand,*
>   *till I lay thy adversaries*
>   *as a footstool under thy feet.*
> *The Lord of Sion extends the staff of thy strength.*
> *Rule in the midst of thine adversaries!*

This Old Testament way of speaking may seem strange to us at first. Can we recognize the Christ in this warlike figure of a victorious King? Does He not renounce just this, that his followers should fight for His Kingdom with the sword? But in the end He also does fight and conquer—only on a higher level. To deliver Himself without resistance to crucifixion, and precisely through His own self-giving to win the hearts of men to a discipleship in freedom—this is His way of fighting. "For this purpose was the Son of God manifested, that He might destroy the works of the devil." (1 John 3; 8.) But He fights in His own special way. The "stakes" and the heroism are truly not less than in a "real" war.

The picture of the victorious Messiah with his enemies under his feet is also one which must be translated out of the Old Testament. What a man overcomes is put "beneath him". Thus it belongs to that which carries him in life, which gives him ground under his feet. That which opposes us gains significance precisely when it is overcome.

* * *

The second section has a quite different ring. The strong, warlike pictures completely disappear. Secrets of the future shine, with a promise of blessing. On the other hand they are still veiled, so that this second part has proved particularly puzzling to commentators. They are only understandable from a Christian angle.

> Thy people—wholly willing
>   in the day of full unfolding of Thy Power.
> They shine in sacred vestments.
> Thy disciples come to thee like dew
>   out of the womb of the morning.
> The Lord hath sworn,
>   and will not repent:
> Thou art a priest for ever
>   after the order of Melchizedek.

The Messiah, the Bringer of Healing, fights and conquers through sacrifice of Himself. The King is also Priest. His priesthood has been granted Him by God through a solemn oath. We are reminded of the 2nd Psalm. There also the poet, David, is raised to a higher world where he can receive divine inspiration. "I will declare a rune of the Lord. He said to me, 'Thou art my son. This day have I begotten thee'." It is as though the inward, divine Mystery of the birth of the Son echoes in the soul of the Psalmist out of the higher spiritual worlds. The emergence of the Son, in whom the Father places his "Thou" over against Himself, is a divine process which is above all temporality; it is a process in the timeless "today" of eternity. It is "the Son born in eternity". "My Son—Thou." So it stands unequivocally in the original text. The Son is enabled to reveal His "I", because the Father has said "Thou" to Him. The background of the "I am" spoken by the Son is the "Thou art" of the Father.

Just as in the 2nd Psalm David hears in heaven that eternal acknowledgment of Sonship, so in the whisper of the 110th Psalm he hears the acknowledgment of Priesthood: "Thou art a priest for ever." The Son, the "Thou" who has emerged from the depths of the Father-being, makes the true divine use of His Ego-hood. He turns to the Father in sacrifice. The Son who brings the offering is the High Priest of the Universe. Sacrifice is His primal, free activity, yet He does not lay claim to it as such. He feels it as given by the Father. Thus in St. John's Gospel Christ speaks of the "work which Thou hast given me". So His priestly activity rests on the foundation of this acknowledgment: "Thou art a priest for ever".

These words are described in the Psalms as "sworn" by God. When a man swears, he calls upon the presence of God as a strengthening for his own words. But God cannot swear by anyone but Himself. So this word-picture of God swearing means perhaps something like this: that God strengthens Himself in Himself, in an inner concentration of His own divine Being. The priesthood of the Son is founded upon this powerful affirmation and concentration. God will never "repent" of this oath, it is the unchangeable, eternal basis for the work of the Son, who is active in the Becoming, in the Offering and in the Transubstantiation of His priesthood.

"After the order of Melchisedek." Through that high Priest-King a pure Sun ritual was once brought to Abraham, in the emblems of bread and wine. With the name of Melchisedek a whole stream of human history is conjured up, which will come to its climax in the historic deed of sacrifice of the Son on Golgotha.

The Christ wills to raise the human beings who accept Him to the same rank of son. They are to grow from childhood to sonship. This also means that he wishes to draw them into co-operation in His priestly activity. They are not merely to watch His deed of Salvation from outside; they are to take part themselves in the continued working out of this deed. Thus when the sacrifice of Christ comes to new life in individual Christians, the general priesthood of all believers comes into being. In this way the "nation" belongs to the Messiah, as the Psalm says in the original text, literally: "Thy nation—freedoms of will". The word "freedom of will" appears in the plural! Christ's nation is not a "mass" who blindly obey a dictator, but a coming together of free personalities. Roger Williams, the noble seventeenth century pioneer of religious freedom in America said, "Christ's true followers are volunteers".

The people of Christ, who have joined together out of pure individual freedom and free will, shine forth in holy vestments. As human beings they have cleansed their supersensible aura. In the words of the Apocalypse, they have "washed their robes in the blood of the Lamb". The Psalm knows very well that this can only become reality "in the day of His victory", at that moment of time when the power of Christ within man will come to its fulfilment.

This "christened" humanity appears at the same time as "youth". "Out of the womb of the morning comes the dew of thy youth." Future mankind is rejuvenated from above. It has overcome the cleverness of worldly old age in the Christian "world festival of youth", and its life is renewed as the freshness of an early dawn. What happens within these human beings cannot be understood through mere earthly, materialistic thinking. Rejuvenation through the spirit remains a riddle to intellectual comprehension. The Psalm speaks of "dew". When a meadow is wet with rain, everyone has seen the dark clouds from which the heavy drops have fallen. But dew comes unseen, unnoticed, in the holy hours of early dawn. The dew emerges mysteriously from the unseen. It is born as it were etherically "from the womb of the morning". The soul-stirring power of the "aurora", the rosy light of dawn, has been deeply felt right up to the time of Jacob Boehme, and of Goethe's "Faust". The rejuvenation of Man comes down to the earth like dew from the heavenly super-sensible world, in a new dawn.

* * *

The third part leads back into the rough, warlike world of the first:

> The Lord at thy right hand
> shatters Kings in the day of His wrath.
> His judgment of the nations
> leaves many corpses behind.
> He will shatter the heads over many lands.
> He will drink of the brook on the way.
> Therefore He will lift up the head.

The prophetic, apocalyptic vision is directed towards future catastrophes. As the Christ will not force men to accept salvation, but allows the full fruitfulness of His deed of healing to depend on their free acceptance of it, it cannot be otherwise than that there will also be rejection. And this rejection will by inner necessity lead to catastrophes. A humanity which shuts itself off from the divine love finally rages against itself. It sets in motion the iron necessities which are rooted in the eternal being of God. Whoever sows mistrust, reaps mistrust. Whoever sows hate, reaps hate. Whoever sows death, reaps death. In so far as this law is founded on the justice of God, God brings these catastrophes; but it is human beings who "ask for them". The destruction which Man brings into the world must hit back on himself in the end—unless he finds refuge in Christ. But wherever Christ's deed of salvation is not able to work, through Man's own rejection, there necessity must work. In this sense we can understand it when the Psalm says of God, that "He fills the earth with corpses". This terrible vision of many dead bodies can already be recognized today much more deeply in all its horror than in David's time.

The work of annihilation also strikes back on "Kings" and on "the heads of many lands". Here we have to think less of political dictators—though perhaps these also—than on the intelligence and sovereign powers of Man in general, which are becoming more and more the rulers of our mechanized lives. Do not we modern readers recognize in "the heads over many lands, all over the earth" the overwhelming intellectual powers of the human head?

But the "head" is not only mentioned negatively. Certainly, the head which rules the earth in loveless, cold, and godless intellectuality will be "shattered". But that which lives in the head of Man can also be included in the work of salvation. Through the power of Christ, intelligence can also turn towards the supersensible, it can be transformed from mere cleverness into wisdom. Then there comes about what the Bible calls the "lifting up of the head". Just "because" the Saviour has drunk "of the brook on the way"—which surely means that He has bent down deeply to the earth—just because of that He is able to bring about "the lifting up of the head".

The New Song

PSALM 96

Again and again the religion of the Old Testament points beyond its own confines. The 96th Psalm issues into the message of Advent: "He comes". It begins by speaking of the "New Song".

"O sing unto the Lord a new song." (A.V.) It is regrettable that this line has lost some of its freshness through ecclesiastical use. We must listen to it as if it were said for the first time, and ask for its concrete meaning. The "new song"—"new" signifies here more than just something different from the old. The "new song" belongs to the same realm as: "the New Testament in My blood"; "a new commandment I give unto you"; "behold, I make all things new".

"New" has a particular relationship to Christ. It is linked with the mystery of the I am. In the "I" we meet the original wellspring of a human being, his uniqueness, which is singular and irreplaceable. In each "ego" the world is mirrored in a unique manner, life assumes a special colour not repeated anywhere else, a "new" sound, special and unrepeatable, is heard. Through Christ this egoity of man is purified from self-seeking and trans-figured into the pattern of the creative Ego, the higher Self, from which the divine life rises ever youthful, unspoiled, fresh and "new". In the en-christened ego the world is constantly re-created from the source of everlasting renewal.

It may have been inevitable that in pre-Christian ages at times the pessimism should be felt which is voiced in Ecclesiastes. "Vanity of vanities; all is vanity." And side by side with it the saying, "There is no new thing under the sun". Both belong to-gether. Something like the negative pole, the negative opposite

175

to Christianity was felt and suffered in those ages. But this, too, was part of the preparation. The church Fathers were right when they claimed that the Incarnation of the Son of God was *the* new thing under the sun. Not before, but with it life acquired meaning, and the ego a creative quality. Now it is no longer true that "all is vanity", senseless and useless, but now everything points towards the great transformation. "Behold, I make all things new." The "new song" is the great hymn of transformation, the song of the renewal of the world.

The Revelation of St. John says of this song of renewal that it can only be sung by those who have been touched by the blood of Christ (14; 3). Only those are able to "learn" the new song.

Psalm 96 in which the sunlike being of Christ is felt, mediated as it were through the Lord Yahweh, speaks in a universally human manner of the "heathen" to whom the glory of the Lord shall be proclaimed. The heathen would go on with the singing of the "old song"; they are still under the spell of the ancient religion in which the Gods spoke through nature and natural event. But he who continues to seek for God in the old direction, in outward manifestations, is in danger of looking for Him where He is no longer to be found. God will now reveal Himself in the innermost being, in the "I". For this reason the Psalm must refer to the heathen Gods as "non-entities". But the existence of other "Gods" is not simply denied. In the Christian conception they would be placed among the celestial hierarchies in their several ranks. But "the Lord is exalted above all Gods"—who therefore are thought to exist. Similarly in some other Psalms: He is "A great king above all Gods" (Ps. 95; 3), "Thou art exalted far above all Gods" (Ps. 97; 9). The sun and his glory which the heathen worshipped outwardly in the cosmos, shall now be found in the God Who speaks the I AM.

> *O sing to the Lord a song of new beginnings.*
> *Sing unto the Lord, all the earth.*
> *Sing unto the Lord.*
> *Proclaim his Name with power and blessing.*

Declare his healing deeds from day to day.
Speak of his light and glorious revelation
To all those still spell-bound by Nature,
Of his wonders to all nations.
For the Lord is great and full of glory,
His dread majesty is above all gods.
The tribal gods have lost their meaning.
But the Lord Who says I AM made the heavens.

The whole of humanity is exhorted to find this God Who carries the secret of the "I". The Psalm knows of a ritual which is celebrated in higher worlds as a pattern and type for all ritual services on earth. Whilst in Psalm 29, where the heavenly ritual is also known, we are shown the "sons of God" (benē elim) serving as priests in the temple of God, in Psalm 96 we are taken a step further. Human beings, too, shall now grow worthy to celebrate the heavenly act. Human beings are to become priestly. Like the angels, they should reveal God with their entire being. Fallen man does not reveal God in his being, he obscures, he hides Him, and celebrates only too often the Service of the Adversary. "Come into his fore-courts." Through his estrangement from God man has been so much absorbed into profane and secular things that he can only gradually get used again to a living together with divine worlds and to the manners which are required: awe, devotion, reverence. It is impossible to enter straightaway from the secular world into the Holy of Holies. It is only pathetic if some modern theologians swallow completely the modern material world picture and then begin simply to talk about "God". There are "fore-courts" and they have their significance.

The "sacred array" which the priestly soul wears in the "sanctuary", is the reflection of the divine radiance mirrored in the devout worshipper. Fallen man saw that he was naked. The shame of nakedness is present wherever nothing but the material body of man is known, and the higher, finer, luminous members of his being are unknown, which in reality clothe him. Admitted again into the sanctuary man catches the divine splendour in

the illumination of the supersensible vestments of his soul and
spirit.

> His countenance radiates the light of revelation;
>   majestic is his mien.
> Power and beauty and dignity fill his sanctuary.
> Bring your offerings to the Lord O you kindreds of
>   the people,
> Be a mirror that reflects his Name,
> Bring your gifts, and enter his forecourts.
> Worship the Lord in the radiant array of priesthood,
> Let the whole earth stand in awe of Him.

A far-off future perfection is anticipated in this vision. But
before this can be achieved, something else has to be done. Man
cannot enter the sanctuary on his own authority and volition. If
he is to be saved from his exile in the secular world, God must
come to meet him. Before man can enter the Kingdom of God,
God enters the world of man. This event took place in Christ.
Our Psalm is inspired by the expectation of the Messiah. The
writer knows that a gracious development has begun, an act of
grace moving towards humanity. "He comes." He "has assumed
His Kingship". (The Hebrew does not simply say, "the Lord
reigneth", but He has *become* king, something real has happened.)
His light begins to shine in the realm in which the power of the
ego in man is destined to rule as a king.

The drawing near of the divine I AM, Who wills to be active
in the Kingdom of man's free personality, affects the whole cosmos. Though the new God will be received in the inwardness of
human hearts, He will radiate from there into all the world and
extend salvation also to the creature. Although the Festival of
Advent can only be begun in the inwardness of the soul, its
significance reaches beyond man.

The Psalm finds wonderful references to nature. We sense the
atmosphere of Advent and Christmas, when "the trees of the
forest" are mentioned. It is as if from the rustling of the trees the
call is born which represents the climax of this Psalm and which

is significantly repeated in powerful rhythms: "For He comes.
For He comes".

> Let it be said among those still spell-bound by Nature:
> The Lord has begun to wield the royal power of the I AM,
> The I AM has become king.
> It is He Who has given firm ground to the earth that it may
>   rest secure.
> He will lead the people in a straight course.
> Let the heavens rejoice, let the earth be glad.
> Let the sea and all that the sea contains make thunderous
>   applause.
> Let the fields be joyful and all the fruit they bear.
> Let the trees in the forest sing for joy.
> For He comes. For He comes.
> He will receive the earth into the order of God,
> He will show right ways to all the world
> And will say Amen to all that is true.

Advent

PSALM 24

I

To the Lord the earth and its fullness,
The round world and they that dwell thereon.
For He hath established it upon the surging seas,
Above swelling floods hath he founded it.

A terse and majestic style is characteristic of this Psalm. "To the Lord the earth." This is primarily an assertion. The earth belongs to Him. It belongs to Him by right, for he Has created it, has founded it in solidity. The earth was not always so hard and solid. The hardness of its rocks is not a matter of course. In primeval times it had still a different physical condition. From a supersensible origin it progressed through fine etheric modes of existence, becoming ever more material. The finer the substance of which the earth once consisted, the more alive it still could be. Pulsating with streams of life, breathed through by divine creative impulses—that was the condition of the earth in primeval times. Even as rigid ice forms out of the moving water that answers each lightest breath of wind with delicate ripples, so, too, did the earth pass from flowing life to a state of rigidity in order to become at last really "earth". For its name, with deep significance, is derived from the solid element (cf. remarks to Psalm 104). Its densification has reached its limit, it can never become harder than stone. It is no longer the living Mother Earth of former days; the state of life that it once possessed as a whole is now continued in the separate living creatures. The hardening of the earth came about for the sake of man. Called to self-reliance and freedom, man needs hard resistance as the hammer needs the anvil, in order to be able to possess himself inwardly as an ego-being. The forming of the solid ground for man was the work of the God Who willed the ego.

But with the solidifying of the earth another possibility arose. The world was no longer filled by direct divine life. Man could thus become a stranger to his heavenly origin and liable to the influence of the powers of the adversary. Thus through a humanity making itself increasingly independent of heaven, a kingdom could gradually arise upon earth of the un-godlike, in fact of the anti-godlike to such a degree that Christ himself described the adversary as the "Prince of this world". Had not the Tempter said in the wilderness, "All this power (*exousia*) will I give thee and all glory, for that is delivered unto me; and to whomsoever I will, I give it. If thou wilt worship me, all shall be thine." (St. Luke 4; 6 and 7.) Man has made himself independent on earth, and the adversary, by way of the human beings he has drawn into his influence, tries to gain ever surer control of the earthly world and break off the whole human earthly kingdom from the divine in order to make it his own. As yet he has had no final success but this whole process of gradually separating out a world estranged from God is at work. It rests with man as to whether the adversary achieves his purpose or not. God has appeared anew upon earth in Christ that He may, in love for him, win man's freedom, and through man win back the earth, too, for the heavens. The Psalm only receives its full meaning through Christ. The sentence "To the Lord the earth" is then no longer just a declaration that it belongs to Him. Rather is this something that must be newly brought about. The earth is to be brought back again to the Divine from which it has so largely fallen away, through those human beings who offer their worship to the true God and not to the "Prince of this world".

That the earth is no longer the property of God as ostensibly as the heavens, is not a concept foreign to the Psalms. In Psalm

115; 16, we read, "The heavens of the heavens (belong) to the Lord but the earth hath he given to the sons of men".

Against this background the first sentence of the 24th Psalm is no longer the statement of an undisputed fact; it acquires the character of a wish. "The earth to the Lord!" becomes a dedication, a consecration, an offering. Man, to whom the earth was given for a "playground", places this playground of his independence again at the disposal of God in freely resolved sacrifice. He will help through his devotion to re-establish the kingdom of God, and wrest the earthly sphere from the adversary. All sacrifice rests fundamentally upon this knowledge: the world is God's from the beginning, it belongs to Him, and yet again it does not belong to Him; I use my human freedom to make Him again the full possessor of His own possession in that I bring Him His own as an offering.

II

Here the Psalm seems to make a direct break and to turn to a completely different subject with no real transition. But there is an unspoken link. If we see a dedicated offering in the sentence, "The earth to the Lord!" we assume that the earth no longer belongs as a matter of course to the kingdom of God, and we realize that the Fall of Man has taken place. Now the human being, filled with longing, strives once more towards the Divine from his fallen state. The second part of the Psalm speaks of this endeavour.

> *Who shall ascend up to the hill of the Lord?*
> *Who shall stand in his holy place?*

All "elevations" of man to God were originally a partial overcoming of the Fall. The mountains soar upwards as symbol of "exalted" human states. Many of them were therefore guarded as holy mounts, the mounts of God known to all religions. Thus Moses was able to meet God on the holy mount and receive his revelation. Similar great men were the teachers of pupils who sought their guidance by leaving lower things behind and ascending to the "hill of God" and the "dwellings" of God to be found there. "This is the generation of them that ask for him, that seek thy face, thou God of Jacob." Psalm 73 uses the expression "the generation of thy sons", and in a similar way our Psalm speaks of the generation of those that seek God's countenance. These men form together something like an Order. They are in reality an invisible community all over the earth, a *communio sanctorum*. Since the place of His holiness is on the heights of the holy mount, he who will lift himself to this experience must satisfy certain conditions, must be purified in thoughts, words and deeds. It is not enough to find the strength to ascend. Having reached the heights man must now also be able to "stand" before God's face—which means, however, with-stand, endure. Without previous purification, he would be annihilated; he could not maintain his own consciousness. It is only "in Christ" that man will be able fully to maintain his transmuted, Christ-permeated ego in the divine world. He then possesses an ego-consciousness not only when he lives on earth in the solitary cell of the material body, but he may also carry it into existence as "spirit among spirits".

The question, "Who shall ascend . . .?" has a parallel in the 15th Psalm. It says there, "Lord, who shall be guest in thy tent? Who shall dwell on the hill of thy holiness?" "Tent"—one should remember the tabernacles, the "tent of his presence"—is the expression for the immediate, almost "densified", presence of God. With the "being guest" is connected the being fed "at the table of the Lord", the mystery of the Communion; and the "dwell" corresponds to the Johannine "abide". This is more than the temporary state of being a guest. The man who dwells on the holy hill (Peter speaks on the Mount of the Transfiguration of building tabernacles) has now become a citizen of the higher world again. The Epistle to the Hebrews speaks of this (12; 22): "Ye have found entry to Mount Sion, and to the city of the living God, the heavenly Jerusalem, and to an innumerable company

of angels, to the fully assembled church of the first-born, whose
names are written in heaven, to God the Judge of All, to the Spirits
of just men made perfect, and to Jesus, the Mediator of the new
Covenant . . ."

In these questions and answers theological commentators have
rightly glimpsed an echo of the ancient ritual of question and
answer at the portals of the sanctuaries. The Priest as "guardian
of the threshold" gave such answers to one who came to a temple
and desired admittance. In such ritualistic usage we recognize
the shadow of the ancient Mysteries. The answer to the question,
"Who shall ascend . . .?" runs:

> He that hath clean hands and a pure heart,
> Who hath not lifted up his soul unto vanity nor
> sworn deceitfully,
> He shall receive the blessing from the Lord,
> And righteousness from the God who helps him.
> This is the generation of them that ask for him
> That seek thy face, O God of Jacob.
>
> Selah.

He who satisfies the demands and is pure in thoughts, words
and deeds ("pure heart, no deceit, clean hands") shall receive
blessing and righteousness. This blessing is the love from above
that crowns the aspirations from below. The efforts for purification are answered by the light of grace from above, even as
the Consecration follows the Offering. The "righteousness"
referred to is obviously not an expression of the perfect moral
qualities possessed by him who aspires to enter the sanctuary.
Man's endeavour must always await completion through the
love from above. Righteousness here is endowment by grace
with the very being of goodness. Experiences of purification, of
"catharsis", are concealed in the challenging words of the stern
Guardian of the Threshold.

A particular note is sounded in the words, "the generation of
those that seek God's face", coming as they do at the end of the

second part of Psalm 24. He who has found the way to the holy
mount and its gifts of grace no longer stands alone, but knows
that he now belongs to a spiritual community. The old commu-
nities were formed through ties of blood, determined through the
body. To "ask" after the Divine and to seek God's face—this
places one in a new community, which has its bond of union in
the spirit.

The Psalm is still restricted to the "God of Jacob". But that
does not prevent us, in the manner of the early Christians, from
thinking of the true "Israel" of the Christian Church, which was
built on the twelvehood of the Apostles and was to include men
of every type under heaven. We may remember, too, that the
God of Jacob is the God who revealed himself in the sublime
dream in which the angels ascend and descend on the heavenly
ladder, and in the prayer at the scene of wrestling by the ford.
("I will not let thee go except thou bless me".)

The dream was dreamed at Beth-El (House of God), the fight
was fought at Peni-El (Countenance of God). Our Psalm has as
its theme the finding of the way to the house and to the countenance of God.

III

The concluding part now follows, and again with no apparent
transition:

> Lift up your heads, O ye gates!
> Lift up, ye portals of eternity!
> The King of glory shall come in.
> Who is the King of glory?
> It is the Lord, a mighty hero,
> The Lord, a hero in battle.

Commentators see in these verses a festival liturgy, perhaps
an alternating chant of two choirs at the solemn reception of the
Ark of the Covenant returning from victorious battle. That may

have been the historical motive for the composition of the Psalm. A more far-reaching truth, however, is expressed in it.

The Psalm celebrates the entry of the approaching God. An important apocalyptic motif is thus introduced. How can the God "come"? Is He not already the omnipresent, filling all things? How then can He come when He is already there? Or is He perhaps after all not completely there, on the earth?

What we have said about the first part of the Psalm gives the key to this problem. We saw that the earthly realm no longer belongs unequivocally to the Divine. This does not, of course, imply that God is not present on earth. He is everywhere. But there are degrees of His presence. His presence is so to speak, more condensed in the heavenly sanctuaries of the higher world than on earth. Where a crime is committed, for instance, God in a certain sense is not there; for if He were completely present, not even the thought of a crime could ever arise. "The earth hath he given to men"; He has left it and has withdrawn from it His full presence in order that man might have space for his freedom. Such an assumption makes it possible to speak of a "coming of God".

This re-entering of God into the earthly sphere which had fallen into the possession of the Prince of this world, began with the appearance of Christ. It was done in such a manner as not to impinge on man's freedom. The Cross is the mystery of the "powerless God" who unfolds, through renouncing the power of compulsion, might of another order through the power of his sacrificial love. The power issuing from the Mystery of Golgotha does not achieve redemption in an automatic fashion. Men are not redeemed through it whether they will or no. In every instance man must set this redemption in motion through his free assent; in other words, for redemption to become effective, Man's "faith" is required. The gradual re-entering of the divine into the earthly world is a process in stages. The "coming" began with Christ becoming Man. It continues with mankind becoming Christian. Gradually we are to become capable of beholding Christ's etheric Light-form. He himself gave the promise that He will come again in *gloria*—that is to say, in radiant etheric light. This coming is the ever-increasing realization of the presence of Christ on earth. His presence will become "denser" and more undeniable, until finally it is directly perceived supersensibly. This "return" in the "clouds of heaven" which begins gradually and is fully realized through long epochs of time, brings with it a judgment. As the reality of Christ becomes increasingly evident, we are more and more seriously faced with the question as to what use we shall make of our freedom, whether we shall respond with Yes or No; whether we shall serve Him or the Prince of this world.

This "coming" of God into the earthly world is foreshadowed in the Old Testament. A series of seven Psalms centre round the theme of the re-established kingdom of Jahve (47, 93, 95, 96, 97, 98, 99): "the Lord has become King". It is prophesied that the Divine will prevail again in the realm of the earth. So we read in Psalm 95, "O come let us worship and bow down, let us kneel before the Lord . . . To-day if ye will hear his voice, harden not your heart . . ." Psalm 96 begins with the apocalyptic motive of the "new Song" (cf. Rev. 5; 9 and 14; 3). "Sing unto the Lord a new song . . . say among the peoples: the Lord has become King." The sentence *Jahve malakh* which is to be found in all these seven Psalms, does not mean "The Lord reigneth" but "He has become King". It is not a matter of announcing something that has always been there. It means rather a changing of the world situation which is prophetically represented as having already begun. Some commentators have assumed that there was a festival celebrating Jahve's mounting of the throne, at which these Psalms would have been sung. This is possible, but then this feast would in fact have had an apocalyptic character of prophetic anticipation, and the wider significance of these Psalms would not be lessened thereby.

The Book of Revelation says: "The kingdoms of this world are become the kingdoms of our Lord and of his Christ" (Rev. 11; 15—at the sounding of the seventh trumpet). And the Elders fall down before the throne and say, "We give thee thanks . . .

because thou hast taken to thee thy great power and hast become king". All this has only a meaning within the framework of a mighty world-drama in which God's rulership on earth is challenged and ultimately re-established. The time has come to recognize that this world drama is not "mythology" of childish peoples, but the only possible interpretation of the world as it really is.

It is only with this train of thought that we are in a position to do justice to the 24th Psalm.

"Lift up your heads, O ye gates! Lift up, ye portals of eternity!" (Thus literally in the original.) The gate presupposes a dividing wall. The higher world is separated as if by a wall from the hardened earthly sphere, shutting itself into itself. And therefore we are not immediately able to "see" and "enter" the kingdom of God (John 3; 3 and 5). But there are gates through which the separated spheres may yet come into some relationship. We speak of the "gate of birth" and the "gate of death", where the threshhold is crossed both hither and thither. So the Psalm speaks here of the portals of eternity. The Hebrew *pitheche olam* is, literally, "primeval, aeon-old portals". This does not change the sense, for the entrance to the higher worlds can be compared to age-old temple gates. These gates are to lift themselves up; a great figure wishes to pass through them. The King of Glory, *kābôd*, is the king of glorious revelation, of etheric light. In the universal symbolism of the ancient civilizations the king was the earthly representative of the divine "I AM" which is the prototype of all royal bearing and dignity. "Thou sayest that I am a king" (John 18; 37). The king of glory who will enter our earthly realm through the portal of eternity—this is the Old Testament's prophecy of the Christ who was to come.

The proclamation of His coming is answered by the question, "Who is this King of Glory?" The question is put for the clarifying of man's consciousness. It is a matter of discerning spirits. Lucifer, too, can show himself as an angel of light. There is an old phrase—*Christus verus luciferus*—Christ is the true Light-bearer. In Lucifer's realm light is glittering illusion; with Christ it is the Light of Life (John 18; 12). The search for discriminating knowledge lies in the question. The Psalm spoke earlier of the generation of those who "ask" concerning Him.

And the answer is "It is the Lord, a mighty hero, a hero of battle". The Lord who speaks the I AM a hero of battle? Are we not still involved in the times of ancient Israel, when one hoped for victory in battle from Jahve? The Psalmist may, in the first place, have meant this. But this does not hinder us from lifting the abiding truth from the historical background. Christ is assuredly not a fighter who uses physical power to subdue others. He makes no consuming fire come down upon the in-hospitable village of the Samaritans (St. Luke 9; 54). He lets his adversaries scoff: "If thou be the Son of God, come down from the cross." But He waits for man to recognize His power as of another order which works in fact through sacrifice, in the "white magic" of Love. This is the nature of His fight against the Prince of this world. He does not fight in the way in which alone fighting could formerly be imagined. He says to Peter, "Put up thy sword into the sheath". And yet He is in the highest sense a fighter, a "hero of the battle". He confronts the brutal "might of the adversary" with the saving power of His Love. The confronting of these two powers is the greatest fight in the world. All other conflicts are but allegory. "Powerful and strong is he who was born at Christmas", sings an old song. So, rightly understood, the Christ is after all the great warrior, the Sun Hero. In St. John's Gospel He sums up His work in these words: "I have overcome the world". (*Nenikeka; nike*—the victory.) This word "won the victory", or "overcome", occurs right through the Apocalypse. "Even as I also overcame . . ." (3; 21). "Behold the Lion hath won the victory . . . and I beheld and lo, a Lamb . . ." (5; 5 and 6). He is the Sun Hero, the Lion, but in the form of the Lamb which sacrifices itself.

What follows, therefore, is fully justified: "It is the Lord, a mighty hero, a hero of the fight".

The knowledge of the Coming One cannot be assimilated with a single proclamation, so it is again repeated as question and answer:

> *Lift up your heads, O ye Gates!*
> *Lift up, ye portals of eternity!*
> *The King of Glory shall come in.*
> *Who is this King of Glory?*
> *It is the Lord of Hosts,*
> *He is the King of Glory!*

We notice a slight alteration in this repetition. This time he is not called "a mighty hero, a hero of the fight", but "the Lord of Hosts". The returning Christ who becomes manifest in etheric light brings with Him at the same time a new knowledge of the supersensible worlds in every detail and variety. The consciousness of man opens again into the supersensible. Together with the Christ the realms of the angels, of the hierarchies, enter again into perceptive consciousness. This is plainly expressed by Christ in his promise to return ". . . when he (the Son of Man) shall come in his own light of revelation (*Doxa, Gloria*) and in that of the Father and of the holy angels" (Luke 9; 26). "But when the Son of Man shall come in his glory and all angels with him . . ." (Matt. 25; 31). In the words, "Ye shall see the heavens open and the angels of God ascending and descending upon the Son of Man" (John 1; 51), Christ promises the return of Jacob's dream of the heavenly ladder in the form of a new perception of the angelic worlds.

Twice does Psalm 24 make the proclamation of the Coming One. In the parallelism of Hebrew poetry the same thing is often repeated twice or more in different words and, as we have it here, the second time can show a slight change of meaning and an advancement. The first time it is "the hero of the fight". This is fulfilled through the Deed of Golgotha, the overcoming of death. The second time it is "the Lord of Hosts" (*Sabaoth*). This is true especially for the "coming again" in the etheric light which is accompanied by a new revelation of the angelic hierarchies.

We can now review the whole Psalm. It consists of three apparently disconnected parts. Part I speaks of the solidifying of the earth, which involves the human problem though this is not expressly stated. It is implied in the dedication "to the Lord the earth!" Part II speaks of man estranged from God and his endeavour to reach again the holy heights. "Who shall ascend to thy holy hill?" Part III is filled by what comes from above to meet wrestling man. If in Part II the movement went from man to God, Part III is dominated by the powerful movement of God towards man, which at the same time is a new approach of the hierarchies to man, as a consequence of the Divine Deed. Man's search for God meets the divine search for man. Thus the inter-connection of the three different parts is brought about as if from a hidden centre.

If we read at the beginning, "To the Lord the earth and the fullness thereof", the answer is found at the end in the proclamation of the Lord who is on the way to man, together with the hosts of heaven (*Sabaoth*).

In Psalm 8, which we considered in the first chapter, the question arose, "What is man?". This question finds a complement in the apocalyptic question, "Who is the King of Glory?".